Rick Steves®

POCKET

FLORENCE

Rick Steves & Gene Openshaw

D0250132

Contents

Introduction

Florence is Europe's cultural capital. As the home of the Renaissance and birthplace of the modern world, Florence practiced the art of civilized living back when the rest of Europe was rural and crude.

Florence is geographically small, with more artistic masterpieces per square mile than anyplace else. In a single day, you can look Michelangelo's *David* in the eyes, fall under the seductive sway of Botticelli's *Birth of Venus,* and climb the modern world's first dome, which still dominates the skyline.

Today's Florence bustles with a modern vibe coursing through its narrow Renaissance lanes. You'll encounter children licking gelato, students riding Vespas, artisans sipping Chianti, and supermodels wearing Gucci—many of the very things you came to Italy to see.

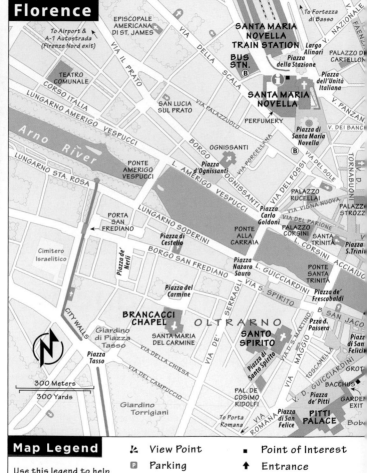

Florence

EPISCOPALE AMERICANA DI ST. JAMES

To Airport & A-1 Autostrada (Firenze Nord exit)

VIA IL PRATO

VIA DELLA SCALA

SANTA MARIA NOVELLA TRAIN STATION

BUS STN.

Largo Alinari

Piazza della Stazione

PALAZZO DI CARTELLON

V. NAZIONALE

V. FAENZA

TEATRO COMUNALE

CORSO ITALIA

LUNGARNO AMERIGO

SAN LUCIA SUL PRATO

VIA PALAZZUOLO

SANTA MARIA NOVELLA

PERFUMERY

Piazza dell'Unità Italiana

V. PANZAN

Arno River

LUNGARNO STA. ROSA

BORGO

OGNISSANTI

Piazza d'Ognissanti

VIA PORCELLANA

L. AMERIGO VESPUCCI

Piazza di Santa Maria Novella

VIA DEL SOLE

VIA DEL FOSSI

V. DEI BANC

PONTE AMERIGO VESPUCCI

Piazza Carlo Goldoni

VIA VIGNA NUOVA

PALAZZO RUCELLAI

VIA DEL PARIONE

PALAZZ STROZZ

TORNABUONI

V. D. PURG

PORTA SAN FREDIANO

LUNGARNO SODERINI

Piazza di Cestello

BORGO SAN FREDIANO

PONTE ALLA CARRAIA

PALAZZO CORSINI

L. CORSINI

SANTA TRINITÀ

Piazza S.Trini

Cimitero Israelitico

Piazza de' Nerli

Piazza Nazaro Sauro

L. GUICCIARDINI

PONTE SANTA TRINITÀ

Piazza de' Frescobaldi

ACCIAIU

CITY WALLS

BRANCACCI CHAPEL

OLTRARNO

VIA DE SERRAGLI

VIA S. SPIRITO

B. SAN JACO

Pza d. Passera

Giardino di Piazza Tasso

SANTA MARIA DEL CARMINE

Piazza del Carmine

SANTO SPIRITO

VIA S. MARTINO

Piazz di San Felici

Piazza Tasso

VIA DELLA CHIESA

VIA DEL CAMPUCCIO

Piazza di Santo Spirito

VIA MAGGIO

TOSCANELLA

D. GUICCIARDINI

GROT

BACCHUS

300 Meters

300 Yards

Giardino Torrigiani

PAL. DE COSIMO RIDOLFI

Piazza de' Pitti

GARDE EXIT

To Porta Romana

VIA ROMANA

Piazza di San Felice

PITTI PALACE

Bob

Map Legend

Use this legend to help you navigate the maps in this book.

- ⅄ View Point
- 🅿 Parking
- 🛈 Tourist Info
- Ⓑ Bus Stop

- ▪ Point of Interest
- ✦ Entrance
- 🆆🅲 Restroom
- Ⓣ Taxi Stand

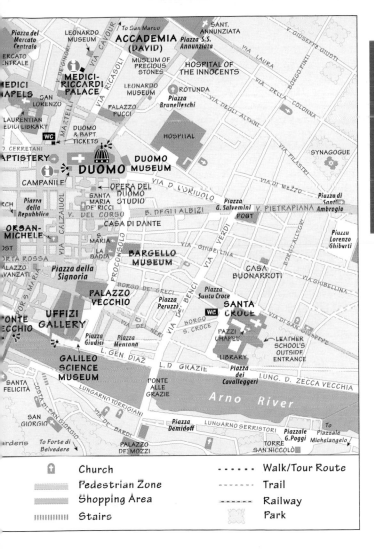

🛐	Church
░░░	Pedestrian Zone
░░░	Shopping Area
⊪⊪⊪	Stairs
· · · · ·	Walk/Tour Route
- - - - -	Trail
⊷⊷⊷⊷	Railway
⬡	Park

About This Book

With this book, I've selected only the best of Florence—admittedly, a tough call. The core of the book is five self-guided tours that zero in on Florence's greatest sights and neighborhoods.

My Renaissance Walk leads you through the historic core—a great introduction to the town's layout, history, and major sights. The Accademia/*David* Tour stars Michelangelo's 17-foot-tall colossus...'nuff said? The Uffizi Gallery Tour presents the world's greatest collection of Italian painting. And at the Bargello and Duomo museums, you'll see some of the world's best sculpture.

The rest of the book is a traveler's tool kit. You'll find plenty more about Florence's attractions, from shopping to nightlife to less touristy sights. And there are helpful hints on saving money, avoiding crowds, getting around town, enjoying a great meal, and more.

Florence by Neighborhood

The best of Florence (population 360,000) lies on the north bank of the Arno River. The main historical sights cluster around the iconic dome of the cathedral (Duomo). Everything is within a 20-minute walk of the cathedral, train station, or Ponte Vecchio (Old Bridge). Much of this historic core is now delightfully traffic-free. For easy orientation, think of Florence divided into sections:

The Duomo to the Arno: The historic spine stretches from the cathedral to the Palazzo Vecchio (with its skyscraping medieval spire) to the Uffizi Gallery to the Ponte Vecchio. It's an easy 10-minute walk along the pedestrian main drag, Via dei Calzaiuoli. Here you'll find major sights, touristy restaurants, and big crowds. My Renaissance Walk is a great introduction to this area.

Key to This Book

Sights are rated:

▲▲▲ **Don't miss**
▲▲ **Try hard to see**
▲ **Worthwhile if you can make it**
No rating **Worth knowing about**

Tourist information offices are abbreviated as **TI,** and bathrooms are **WCs.**

Like Europe, this book uses the **24-hour clock.** It's the same through 12:00 noon, then keeps going: 13:00 (1:00 p.m.), 14:00 (2:00 p.m.), and so on.

For **opening times,** if a sight is listed as "May-Oct daily 9.00-16:00," it should be open from 9 a.m. until 4 p.m. from the first day of May until the last day of October (but expect exceptions).

For **updates** to this book, visit www.ricksteves.com/update. For a valuable list of reports and experiences—good and bad—from fellow travelers, check www.ricksteves.com/feedback.

North of the Duomo: Tourist activities and restaurants revolve around two main centers: the Church of San Lorenzo (museums and nearby markets), and the Accademia (and nearby San Marco Museum).

East of the Duomo: The landmark is the Church of Santa Croce—a major sight and a people-gathering spot. Otherwise, this is a less-touristed area, sprinkled with minor sights, and a few hotels and restaurants.

West of the Duomo: The train station (and bus station)—a 10- to 15-minute walk from the Duomo—form the western border of the historic core. The area is somewhat urban and dreary and there are few sights (besides the church of Santa Maria Novella), but it's convenient for hotels and restaurants.

South of the Arno River (Oltrarno): Less touristed and more local, it's a place of artisan workshops and car traffic. Tourists enjoy the Pitti Palace (and Boboli Gardens) and Brancacci Chapel, as well as local-filled restaurants.

Florence at a Glance

▲▲▲**Accademia** Michelangelo's *David* and powerful (unfinished) *Prisoners*. Reserve ahead or get a Firenze Card. **Hours:** Tue-Sun 8:15-18:50, possibly Tue until 22:00 June-Sept, closed Mon. See page 112.

▲▲▲**Uffizi Gallery** Greatest collection of Italian paintings anywhere. Reserve well in advance or get a Firenze Card. **Hours:** Tue-Sun 8:15-18:50, closed Mon. See page 110.

▲▲▲**Bargello** Underappreciated sculpture museum (Michelangelo, Donatello, Medici treasures). **Hours:** Tue-Sat 8:15-17:00, until 13:50 Nov-March; also open second and fourth Mon and first, third, and fifth Sun of each month. See page 108.

▲▲▲**Duomo Museum** Marvelous cathedral museum with artistic treasures and some of the finest Florentine sculptures. **Hours:** Daily 9:00-20:00, closed first Tue of each month. See page 107.

▲▲**Duomo** Gothic cathedral with colorful facade and the first dome built since ancient Roman times. **Hours:** Mon-Fri 10:00-17:00 (Thu until 16:30), Sat 10:00-16:45, Sun 13:30-16:45. See page 106.

▲▲**Museum of San Marco** Best collection anywhere of artwork by the early Renaissance master Fra Angelico. **Hours:** Tue-Fri 8:15-13:50, Sat 8:15-16:50; also open 8:15-13:50 on first, third, and fifth Mon and 8:15-16:50 on second and fourth Sun of each month. See page 112.

▲▲**Medici Chapels** Tombs of Florence's great ruling family, designed and carved by Michelangelo. **Hours:** Tue-Sat 8:15-17:00 except Nov-March until 13:50; also open second and fourth Mon and first, third, and fifth Sun of each month. See page 114.

▲▲**Palazzo Vecchio** Fortified palace, once the home of the Medici family, wallpapered with history. **Hours:** Museum and excavations open Fri-Wed 9:00-23:00 (Oct-March until 19:00), Thu 9:00-14:00; shorter hours for tower. See page 110.

▲▲**Galileo Science Museum** Fascinating old clocks, telescopes, maps, and Galileo's middle finger. **Hours:** Wed-Mon 9:30-18:00, Tue until 13:00. See page 111.

▲▲**Santa Croce Church** Precious art, tombs of famous Florentines, and Brunelleschi's Pazzi Chapel in 14th-century church. **Hours:** Mon-Sat 9:30-17:30, Sun 14:00-17:30. See page 118.

▲▲**Church of Santa Maria Novella** Thirteenth-century Dominican church with Masaccio's famous 3 D painting. **Hours:** Mon-Thu 9:00-19:00 (Oct-March until 17:30), Fri 11:00-19:00 (Oct-March until 17:30), Sat 9:00-17:30, Sun 13:00-17:30. See page 121.

▲▲**Pitti Palace** Several museums in lavish palace plus sprawling Boboli and Bardini Gardens. **Hours:** Palatine Gallery, Royal Apartments, and Gallery of Modern Art: Tue-Sun 8:15-18:50, closed Mon; Boboli and Bardini Gardens and other museums have similar (but not identical) hours. See page 123.

▲▲**Brancacci Chapel** Works of Masaccio, early Renaissance master who reinvented perspective. **Hours:** Mon and Wed-Sat 10:00-17:00, Sun 13:00-17:00, closed Tue. Reservations required, though often available on the spot. See page 126.

▲▲**San Miniato Church** Sumptuous Renaissance chapel and sacristy showing scenes of St. Benedict. **Hours:** Mon-Sat 9:30-13:00 & 15:30-20:00, until 19:00 off-season, Sun 9:30-20:00. See page 129.

▲**Climbing the Duomo's Dome** Grand view into the cathedral, close-up of dome architecture, and, after 463 steps, a glorious city vista; reservations required. **Hours:** Mon-Fri 8:30-20:00, Sat 8:30-17:40, Sun 13:00-16:00. See page 107.

▲**Campanile** Bell tower with views similar to Duomo's, 50 fewer steps, and no reservations. **Hours:** Daily 8:30-20:00. See page 107.

▲**Baptistery** Bronze doors fit to be the gates of paradise. **Hours:** Doors always viewable; interior open Mon-Sat 8:15-20:00, Sun 8:30-14:00. See page 107.

▲**Medici-Riccardi Palace** Lorenzo the Magnificent's home, with fine art, frescoed ceilings, and Gozzoli's lovely Chapel of the Magi. **Hours:** Thu-Tue 8:30-19:00, closed Wed. See page 116.

▲**Ponte Vecchio** Famous bridge lined with gold-and-silver shops. See page 111.

▲**Piazzale Michelangelo** Hilltop square with stunning view of Duomo and Florence, with San Miniato Church just uphill. See page 129.

Daily Reminder

Sunday: Mercato Centrale is closed (but food court open). The Bargello and Medici Chapels close on the second and fourth Sunday of the month. The Museum of San Marco is closed on the first, third, and fifth Sunday.

    The Baptistery's interior closes early, at 14:00. A few sights are open only in the afternoon: the Duomo and its dome (13:30-16:40), Santa Croce Church (14:00-17:30), Basilica of San Lorenzo (13:30-17:30), Brancacci Chapel (13:00-17:00), and Church of Santa Maria Novella (13:00-17:30).

    The following sights are free and crowded on the first Sunday of the month, and reservations are not available: Uffizi, Accademia, Pitti Palace, Bargello, and Medici Chapels.

Monday: The biggies are closed, including the Accademia (*David*) and the Uffizi Gallery, as well as Pitti Palace's Palatine Gallery, Royal Apartments, and Gallery of Modern Art.

    The Pitti Palace's Boboli and Bardini Gardens and the Argenti/Silverworks Museum close on the first and last Monday. The Museum of San Marco closes on the second and fourth Monday. The Bargello, Palazzo Davanzati, and the Medici

Planning Your Time

Plan your sightseeing carefully to avoid lines and work around closed days. (See my sightseeing tips on page 164.) Florence is so geographically small that, even if you only had one day, you could see the biggies in a 12-hour sightseeing blitz. But let's assume you have at least three days.

Day 1: See the Accademia (*David*)—reserve in advance or get a Firenze Card. Visit the nearby museum of San Marco (Fra Angelico). After lunch, art lovers will want to get a start on Florence's many sights. Choose from the Medici Chapels (Michelangelo), Santa Maria Novella, Palazzo Vecchio, Medici-Riccardi Palace, Pitti Palace, Brancacci Chapel, or Santa Croce. Around 16:30, visit the Baptistery and Duomo interior, or climb the dome or Campanile. In the cool of the evening, take my Renaissance Walk. End with dinner in the old center.

Chapels are closed on the first, third, and fifth Monday. The San Lorenzo Market is closed Monday in winter.

Target these sights on Monday: the Duomo, Duomo Museum, Campanile, Baptistery, Medici-Riccardi Palace, Brancacci Chapel, Mercato Nuovo, Mercato Centrale, Casa Buonarroti, Galileo Science Museum, Palazzo Vecchio, and churches (including Santa Croce and Santa Maria Novella).

Tuesday: Casa Buonarroti and the Brancacci Chapel are closed. The Duomo Museum is closed on the first Tuesday of the month. The Galileo Science Museum closes early (13:00)

Wednesday: The Medici-Riccardi Palace is closed.

Thursday: The following sights close early: Palazzo Vecchio (14:00) and off-season, the Duomo (16:30).

Friday: All sights are open.

Saturday: All sights are open, but the Duomo's dome closes earlier than usual, at 17:40.

Early Closing Warning: Some of Florence's sights close surprisingly early (by 13:50), especially off-season.

Day 2: Start with the Bargello (great statues), then the Galileo Science Museum. After lunch, hit the markets, shop, wander, take a bike or walking tour, or do more museum-going. Around 16:30, see the Uffizi Gallery's unforgettable paintings—reserve well in advance or get a Firenze Card. Then stroll to the Arno, and cross to the Oltrarno for dinner.

Day 3: Start with the Duomo Museum. After lunch, sightsee any leftovers from the first two days. Around 16:00, take a taxi or bus to Piazzale Michelangelo for city views and the San Miniato Church. Walk back into town for dinner.

With more days, you could even fit in a day trip to Siena, Pisa, Lucca, or a Tuscan hill town.

These are busy day-plans, so be sure to schedule in slack time for picnics, laundry, people-watching, leisurely dinners, shopping, and recharging your touristic batteries. Slow down and be open to unexpected experiences and the hospitality of the Italian people.

Trip Tips: Avoid lines by making reservations or buying a Firenze Card, and check opening hours carefully. ∩ Download my free Florence **audio tours**—covering the Renaissance Walk, the Uffizi Gallery, the Bargello, and the Accademia (*David*)—and take them along (see page 165 for details). Do your most intense sightseeing in the morning or late afternoon to avoid heat and crowds. Stop often for gelato.

I hope you have a great trip! Traveling like a temporary local and taking advantage of the information here, you'll enjoy the absolute most out of every mile, minute, and euro. I'm happy that you'll be visiting places I know and love, and meeting some of my favorite Italian people.

Buon viaggio! Happy travels!

Renaissance Walk

From the Duomo to the Arno River

After centuries of labor, Florence gave birth to the Renaissance. We'll start with the soaring church dome that stands as the proud symbol of the Renaissance spirit. Just opposite, you'll find the Baptistery doors that opened the Renaissance. Finally, we'll reach Florence's political center, dotted with monuments of that proud time. Great and rich as this city is, it's easily covered on foot. This walk through the top sights is less than a mile long, running from the Duomo to the Arno River.

This walk gives an overview of the top sights in Florence—if you'd like to visit any of them in depth, ✪ see the Sights chapter for more specifics.

ORIENTATION

Length of This Walk: Allow two hours, including interior visits of the Baptistery and Orsanmichele Church (but not the other sights mentioned).

Getting Into Duomo Sights: You can take this walk without entering any sights, and it's free to enter the Duomo. But seeing any of the Duomo's related sights requires a €15 combo-ticket (sold at ticket office opposite Baptistery entrance at staffed counter and from ticket machines; and at the Campanile, Duomo crypt, and Duomo Museum). Duomo sights are also covered by the Firenze Card, but you must present your card at the ticket office opposite the Baptistery (look for a priority queue) to obtain a free combo-ticket. Reservations are required to climb the dome, even with a combo-ticket or Firenze Card.

Duomo (Cathedral): Free, Mon-Fri 10:00-17:00 (Thu until 16:30), Sat 10:00-16:45, Sun 13:30-16:45. A modest dress code is enforced.

Campanile (Giotto's Tower): Covered by €15 combo-ticket and Firenze Card, daily 8:30-20:00, last entry 40 minutes before closing, 414 steps.

Baptistery: Covered by €15 combo-ticket and Firenze Card. Interior open Mon-Sat 8:15-20:00, Sun 8:30-14:00. Entrance is at the north door. The facsimile bronze doors on the outside are always viewable and free to see.

Climbing the Dome: Covered by €15 combo-ticket and Firenze Card, but you must make a reservation either at the ticket office or online (www.museumflorence.com); Mon-Fri 8:30-20:00, Sat 8:30-17:40, Sun 13:00-16:00, 463 steps.

Orsanmichele Church: Free, daily 10:00-17:00, upstairs museum open Mon only. The replica niche sculptures are always viewable from the outside.

Palazzo Vecchio: Courtyard-free; museum-€10, tower climb-€10, museum plus tower-€14, covered by Firenze Card; museum open Fri-Wed 9:00-23:00 (Oct-March until 19:00), Thu until 14:00 year-round; ticket office closes one hour earlier.

Information: There's a TI right on Piazza del Duomo, and another one a couple of blocks north of the Duomo at Via Cavour 1.

Tours: ⌂ Download my free Renaissance Walk audio tour.

Services: Pay WCs are at the ticket office opposite the Baptistery. You can refill your water bottle at public twist-the-handle fountains at the Duomo (left side, by the dome entrance), Palazzo Vecchio (behind the Neptune fountain), and on Ponte Vecchio.

Eating: You'll find plenty of cafés, self-service cafeterias, bars, and gelato shops along the route. For cheap eats, try **$** Self-Service Ristorante Leonardo or **$$** Cantinetta dei Verrazzano, a bakery/café with good focacce sandwiches (near the Duomo, see page 145). The popular **$** L'Antico Trippaio sandwich cart is a block east of Orsanmichele on Via Dante Alighieri.

Starring: Brunelleschi's dome, Ghiberti's doors, and the city of Florence—old and new.

THE WALK BEGINS

Overview

The Duomo, the cathedral with the distinctive red dome, is the center of Florence and the orientation point for this walk. If you ever get lost, home's the dome. We'll start here, see several sights in the area, and then stroll down the city's pedestrian-only main street to the Palazzo Vecchio and the Arno River. Consider prefacing this walk with a visit to the ultimate Renaissance man: Michelangelo's David (✪ see the Accademia Tour chapter).

Stroll around the piazza in front of the Duomo, and take in the sights. There's the church itself, with its ornate white, green, and pink facade. The Duomo is topped with a soaring dome—though from close up, it's hard to even see the dome because the church itself is so big. To the right of the Duomo rises its skyscraping bell tower (the Campanile). In front of the church is the Baptistery, an octagonal, black-and-white stone building that's bigger than many churches. The

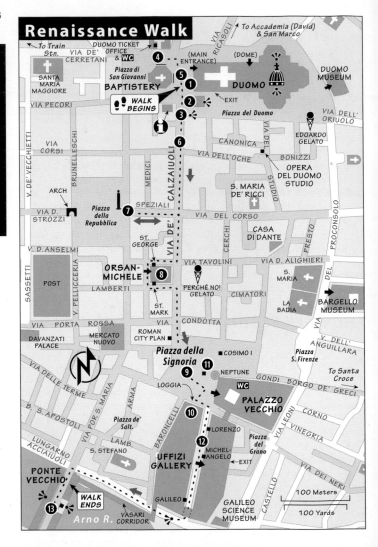

Renaissance Walk Key

1. The Duomo
2. Campanile
3. View of the Dome
4. Baptistery – North Doors
5. Baptistery – East Doors
   (Gates of Paradise)
6. Via de' Calzaiuoli
7. Piazza della Repubblica
8. Orsanmichele Church
9. Piazza della Signoria
10. Loggia dei Lanzi
11. Savonarola Plaque
12. Uffizi Courtyard Statues
13. Ponte Vecchio

piazza is always buzzing with activity—tourists, horse buggies, and Florentines on their way to somewhere else—as this is one of the main intersections in town. Get a feel for the place, then let's explore.

▶ *Stand in front of the Duomo as you get your historical bearings.*

The Florentine Renaissance

In the 13th and 14th centuries, Florence was a powerful center of banking, trading, and textile manufacturing. The resulting wealth fertilized the cultural soil. Then came the Black Death in 1348. Nearly half the population died, but the infrastructure remained strong, and the city rebuilt better than ever. Led by Florence's chief family—the art-crazy Medici—and propelled by the naturally aggressive and creative spirit of the Florentines, it's no wonder that the long-awaited Renaissance finally took root here.

The Renaissance—the "rebirth" of Greek and Roman culture that swept across Europe—started around 1400 and lasted about 150 years. In politics, the Renaissance meant democracy; in science, a renewed interest in exploring nature. The general mood was optimistic and "humanistic," with a confidence in the power of the individual.

In medieval times, poverty and ignorance had made life "nasty, brutish, and short" (for lack of a better cliché). The church was the people's opiate, and their lives were only a preparation for a happier time in heaven after leaving this miserable vale of tears.

Medieval art was the church's servant. The noblest art form was architecture—churches themselves—and other arts were considered most worthwhile if they embellished the house of God. Painting and sculpture were narrative and symbolic, designed to tell Bible stories to the devout and illiterate masses.

As prosperity rose in Florence, so did people's confidence in life and themselves. Middle-class craftsmen, merchants, and bankers felt they could control their own destinies, rather than be at the whim of nature. They found much in common with the ancient Greeks and Romans, who valued logic and reason above superstition and blind faith.

Renaissance art was a return to the realism and balance of Greek and Roman sculpture and architecture. Domes and round arches replaced Gothic spires and pointed arches. In painting and sculpture, Renaissance artists strove for realism. Merging art and science, they used mathematics, the laws of perspective, and direct observation of nature.

This was not an anti-Christian movement. Artists saw themselves as an extension of God's creative powers. The church even supported the Renaissance and commissioned many of its greatest works—for instance, Raphael frescoed images of Plato and Aristotle on the walls of the Vatican. But for the first time in Europe since Roman times, there were rich laymen who wanted art simply for art's sake.

After 1,000 years of waiting, the embers of Europe's classical heritage burst into flames right here in Florence.

The Duomo

Florence's massive cathedral is Florence's geographical and spiritual heart. The dome of Florence's cathedral, visible from all over the city, inspired Florentines to do great things. (Most recently, it inspired the city to make the area around the cathedral delightfully traffic-free.)

Brunelleschi's dome atop the medieval Duomo

The Duomo facade—glorious or gaudy?

The big church itself (called the Duomo) was built in the Middle Ages by architects who left it unfinished.

The church was begun in 1296, in the Gothic style. After generations of work, it was still unfinished. The facade was little more than bare brick, and it stood that way until it was completed in 1870 in the "Neo"-Gothic style. Its "retro" look captures the feel of the original medieval façade, with green, white, and pink marble sheets that cover the brick construction. You'll see Gothic (pointed) arches and three stories decorated with mosaics and statues. This over-the-top facade is adored by many, while others call it "the cathedral in pajamas." The Duomo is dedicated to the Virgin Mary. Find her statue right in the center—above the main doorway but below the round window.

The interior is cavernous and bare with a few noteworthy sights. Entry is free but not worth a long wait. For a brief tour of the interior, see page 106.

▶ Now turn to the church's bell tower, to the right.

Campanile (Giotto's Tower)

The bell tower (to the right of the cathedral's front) offers an easier and faster climb than the Duomo's dome, though the unobstructed views from the Duomo are better. The 270-foot bell tower was begun in the 1300s by the great painter Giotto. As a forerunner of the Renaissance genius, Giotto excelled in many artistic fields, just as Michelangelo would do two centuries later. In his day, Giotto was called the ugliest man to ever walk the streets of Florence, but he designed what many call the most beautiful bell tower in all of Europe.

The bell tower served as a sculpture gallery for Renaissance artists. Find the four statues of prophets (about a third of the way up) done by the great Early Renaissance sculptor, Donatello. The most striking of them is baldheaded Habbakuk.

Closer to ground level are several hexagonal panels that ring the Campanile. These reliefs depict Bible scenes: God Creates Adam, then Eve, and they set to work. Then Jabal learns to till the soil while Jubal blows his horn   and so on. The realism of these groundbreaking works paved the way for Michelangelo and the High Renaissance generations later. (By the way, these are copies—the originals are at the excellent Duomo Museum, just behind the church. There you'll find more statues from the Duomo, plus displays on the dome, Ghiberti's bronze doors, and a late *Pietà* by Michelangelo. ✪ See the Duomo Museum Tour chapter.)

Climbing the Campanile doesn't require a reservation, just a Duomo combo-ticket (see page 107 for information about climbing the tower).

▶ *Now take in the Duomo's star attraction: the dome. The best viewing spot is just to the right of the façade, from the corner of the pedestrian-only Via de' Calzaiuoli.*

View of the Dome

The dome rises 330 feet from ground level. It's made of red brick, held together with eight white ribs, and topped with a lantern.

Think of the confidence of the age: The Duomo was built with a big hole in its roof, just waiting for a grand dome to cover it—but the technology needed to create such a dome had yet to be invented. *Non c'è problema.* The Florentines knew that someone would soon be able to handle the challenge. In the 1400s, the architect Filippo Brunelleschi was called on to finish the job. Brunelleschi capped the church Roman-style—with a tall, self-supporting dome as grand as the ancient Pantheon's (which he had studied).

He used a dome within a dome. First, he built the grand white skeletal ribs, which you can see, then filled them in with interlocking bricks in a herringbone pattern. The dome grew upward like an igloo, supporting itself as it proceeded from the base. When the ribs reached the top, Brunelleschi arched them in and fixed them in place with the lantern at the top. His dome, built in only 14 years, was the largest since Rome's Pantheon.

Brunelleschi's dome was the wonder of the age, the model for many domes to follow, from St. Peter's to the US Capitol. People gave it the ultimate compliment, saying, "Not even the ancients could have done it." Michelangelo, setting out to construct the dome of St. Peter's, drew inspiration from the dome of Florence. He said, "I'll make its sister...bigger, but not more beautiful."

You can climb the dome for Florence's best views, but it requires a reservation, usually in advance (for details, see page 107).

The Baptistery is the small octagonal building in front of the church. If you decide to go inside, you can get a ticket at the office across the piazza (Firenze Card holders need to go to the ticket office to obtain a

11th-century Baptistery, 14th-century church and tower, 15th-century dome, 19th-century facade

free combo-ticket). If you just want to look at the exterior doors, there's no charge, of course.

Baptistery and Ghiberti's Bronze Doors

Florence's Baptistery is dear to the soul of the city. Built in the 11th century, it's Florence's oldest surviving building. In medieval and Renaissance times, the locals—eager to link themselves to the classical past—believed (wrongly) that this was a Roman building. And for a thousand years, most festivals and parades have either started or ended here.

Doors: Some say that these doors actually started the Renaissance. It was the year 1401, and Florence was holding a competition to find the best artist to create the Baptistery's north doors. Florence had strong civic spirit, with different guilds (powerful trade associations) and merchant groups embellishing their city with superb art. All the greats entered the contest, but 24-year-old Lorenzo Ghiberti won easily, beating out heavyweights such as Brunelleschi (who, after losing the Baptistery gig, was free to go to Rome, study the Pantheon, and later build the Duomo's dome). The original entries of Brunelleschi and Ghiberti are in the Bargello, where you can judge them for yourself.

For the next 25 years, Ghiberti worked on these north doors, creating such realistic figures that all of Florence was astounded. But that was just the beginning.

When the Baptistery needed another set of doors, this time there was literally no contest. Ghiberti's bronze panels for the east doors (facing the church) added a whole new dimension to art—depth. Michelangelo said these doors were fit to be the "Gates of Paradise."

Baptistery doors—the "Gates of Paradise"

Jacob and Esau—receding arches create 3-D

Ghiberti's "Gates of Paradise"

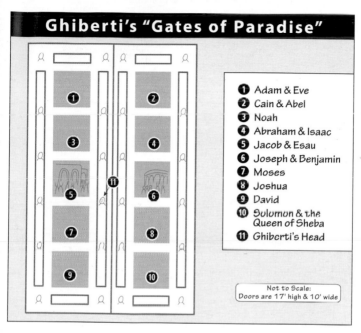

1. Adam & Eve
2. Cain & Abel
3. Noah
4. Abraham & Isaac
5. Jacob & Esau
6. Joseph & Benjamin
7. Moses
8. Joshua
9. David
10. Solomon & the Queen of Sheba
11. Ghiberti's Head

Not to Scale:
Doors are 17' high & 10' wide

(These panels are copies; the originals are in the nearby Duomo Museum. For more detailed descriptions of the panels, see page 90.) Here we see how the Renaissance masters merged art and science. Realism was in, and Renaissance artists used math, illusion, and dissection to create it.

In the Jacob and Esau panel (just above eye level on the left), receding arches, floor tiles, and banisters create a background for a realistic scene. The figures in the foreground stand and move like real people, telling the Bible story with human details. Amazingly, this spacious, 3-D scene is made from bronze only a couple of inches deep.

Find his tiny self-portrait—he's the bald guy in the center of the door frame, atop the second row of panels.

Interior: You'll see a fine example of pre-Renaissance mosaic art (1200s-1300s) in the Byzantine style. Workers from St. Mark's in

Baptistery interior's *Last Judgment* mosaic: Christ gives the ultimate thumbs-up and thumbs-down

Venice came here to make the remarkable ceiling mosaics (of Venetian glass) in the late 1200s.

The Last Judgment on the ceiling gives us a glimpse of the medieval worldview. Life was a preparation for the afterlife, when you would be judged and saved, or damned—with no in-between. Christ, peaceful and reassuring, blesses those at his right hand with heaven (thumbs up) and sends those on his left to hell (the ultimate thumbs-down), to be tortured by demons and gnashed between the teeth of monsters. This hellish scene looks like something out of the *Inferno* by Dante, who was dipped into the baptismal waters right here.

The rest of the ceiling mosaics tell the history of the world, from Adam and Eve (over the north/entrance doors, top row) to Noah and the Flood (over south doors, top row), to the life of Christ (second row, all around) to the life, ministry, and eventual beheading of John the Baptist (bottom row, all around)—all bathed in the golden glow of pre-Renaissance heaven.

▶ *Now head south, entering the pedestrian-only street that runs from here toward the Arno River.*

Via de' Calzaiuoli

The pedestrian-only Via de' Calzaiuoli (kahlts-ay-WOH-lee), the former "street of the stocking makers," is today lined with shops that cater to the mobs of tourists. This street has long been the main axis of the city, and was part of the ancient Roman grid plan that became Florence. In medieval times, this street connected the religious center (where we are now) with the political center (where we're heading), a five-minute walk away. Back then, the shops sold cheese, flags, and horse bridles. Nowadays this historic core is a pleasant place to stroll, people-watch, window-shop, and wonder why American cities can't become more pedestrian-friendly.

▶ *Continue down Via de' Calzaiuoli. Two blocks down from the Baptistery, look right on Via degli Speziali and consider side-tripping to see...*

Piazza della Repubblica

This large square sits on the site of the original Roman Forum. Florence was founded 2,000 years ago as a riverside garrison town, with its main square here where Via Corso and Via Roma met. If you look at a map of Florence today, you can make out the ghost of Rome in its streets: a grid-plan city center surrounded by a circular city wall.

In the 1860s, the square got its magnificent triumphal arch. It celebrated the unification of Italy. In fact, from 1865 to 1870, Florence became the capital of the newly united nation of Italy.

To live up to its role, the city was spiffed up. City walls were taken down, grand European-style boulevards were blasted through, and the Jewish ghetto was razed to create this imposing, modern forum surrounded by stately circa-1890 buildings. Notice the proud statement atop the triumphal arch, which proclaims, "The squalor of the ancient city is given a new life."

For more on this square, see page 109.

▶ *A block farther, at the intersection with Via Orsanmichele, is the...*

Orsanmichele Church—Florence's Medieval Roots

The Orsanmichele Church provides an interesting look at Florentine values. It's a combo church/granary. Originally, this was an open loggia (covered porch) with a huge grain warehouse upstairs. The arches of the loggia were artfully filled in (14th century), and the building gained a new purpose—as a church. This was prime real estate on what had become the main drag between the church and palace.

The 14 niches in the walls feature remarkable-in-their-day statues paid for by the city's rising middle class of merchants and their 21 guilds.

Florence in 1400 was a republic, a government working for the interests not of a king, but of these guilds (much as modern America caters to corporate interests). The guilds commissioned statues as PR gestures, hiring the finest artists of the time. As a result, the statues that ring the church (generally copies of originals stored safely in nearby museums) function as a textbook of the evolution of Florentine art.

Orsanmichele Exterior

In earlier Gothic times, statues were set deep into church niches, simply embellishing the house of God. Here at the Orsanmichele Church, we see statues—as restless as man on the verge of the Renaissance—stepping out from the protection of the Church.

▶ Head up Via Orsanmichele and circle the church exterior counterclockwise to enjoy the statues.

Nanni di Banco's *Quattro Santi Coronati* (c. 1415-1417)

These four early Christians were sculptors martyred by the Roman emperor Diocletian because they refused to sculpt pagan gods. They seem to be contemplating the consequences of the fatal decision they're about to make. Beneath some of the niches, you'll find the symbol of the guilds that paid for the art. Art historians differ here. Some think the work was commissioned by the carpenters' and masons' guild. Others contend it was by the guys who did discount circumcisions.

Donatello's *St. George* (c. 1417)

George is alert, perched on the edge of his niche, scanning the horizon for dragons and announcing the new age with its new outlook. His knitted brow shows there's a drama unfolding. Sure, he's anxious, but he's also self-assured. Comparing this Renaissance-style *St. George* to *Quattro Santi Coronati,* you can psychoanalyze the heady changes under way. This is humanism.

This *St. George* is a copy of the original (now in the Bargello; ✪ see the Bargello Tour chapter).

Orsanmichele—staid late-medieval saints

Donatello's bold, Renaissance *St. George*

▶ *Continue around the corner of the church (bypassing the entrance for now), all the way to the back side.*

Donatello's *St. Mark* (1411-1413)

The evangelist cradles his gospel in his strong, veined hand and gazes out, resting his weight on the right leg while bending the left. Though subtle, St. Mark's twisting *contrapposto* pose was the first seen since antiquity. Commissioned by the linen-sellers' guild, the statue has elaborately detailed robes that drape around the natural contours of his weighty body. When the guild first saw the statue, they thought the oversized head and torso made it top-heavy. Only after it was lifted into its raised niche did Donatello's cleverly designed proportions look right—and the guild accepted it. Eighty years after young Donatello carved this statue, a teenage Michelangelo Buonarroti stood here and marveled at it.

▶ *Backtrack to the entrance and go inside.*

Orsanmichele Interior

Step into Florence circa 1350. The church does not have a typical nave because it was adapted from a granary. Look for the pillars (on the left) with rectangular holes in them about four feet off the ground. These were once used as chutes for delivering grain from the storage rooms upstairs. Look up to see the rings hanging from the ceiling, used to anchor pulleys for either lifting grain or hoisting platforms with candles to act as chandeliers, and the iron bars spanning the vaults for support.

The fanciful tabernacle by Andrea Orcagna was designed exactly for this space: Like the biggest Christmas tree possible, it's capped by an angel whose head touches the ceiling. Take in the Gothic

Donatello's *St. Mark* on Orsanmichele

Gothic tabernacle inside Orsanmichele

tabernacle's medieval elegance. What it lacks in depth and realism it makes up for in color, with an intricate assemblage of marble, glass, gold, and expensive lapis lazuli. Florence had just survived the terrible bubonic plague of 1348, which killed half the population. The elaborate tabernacle was built to display Bernardo Daddi's *Madonna delle Grazie,* which received plague survivors' grateful prayers. While it's great to see art in museums, it's even better to enjoy it in its original setting—"in situ"—where the artist intended it to be seen. When you view similar altarpieces out of context in the Uffizi, think back on the candlelit medieval atmosphere that surrounds this altarpiece.

Upstairs is a free museum (open Mon only) displaying most of the originals of the statues you just saw outside. They represent virtually every big name in pre-Michelangelo Florentine sculpture: Donatello, Ghiberti, Brunelleschi, Giambologna, and more.

Consider returning for one of the church's atmospheric evening concerts; same-day tickets are sold from the door facing Via de' Calzaiuoli (see Orsanmichele Church map). You can also book tickets here for the Uffizi and Accademia.

▶ *The Bargello, with Florence's best collection of sculpture, is a few blocks east, down Via dei Tavolini. (✪ See the Bargello Tour chapter.) But let's continue down the mall 50 more yards, to the huge and historic square called...*

Piazza della Signoria

The main civic center of Florence, Piazza della Signoria is dominated by the Palazzo Vecchio, the Uffizi Gallery, and the marble greatness of old Florence littering its cobbles. Piazza della Signoria still vibrates with the echoes of Florence's past—executions, riots, and great celebrations. There's even Roman history: Look for the chart showing the ancient city (on a waist-high, freestanding display to your right as you enter the square). Today, it's a tourist's world with pigeons, selfie sticks, horse buggies, and tired spouses. If it would make your weary companion happy, stop in at the expensive Rivoire café to enjoy its fine desserts, pudding-thick hot chocolate, and the best view seats in town.

Before you towers the Palazzo Vecchio, the palatial Town Hall of the Medici—a fortress designed to contain riches and survive the many riots that went with local politics. The windows are just beyond the reach of angry stones, and the tower was a handy lookout post. Justice was doled out sternly on this square. Until 1873, Michelangelo's **David** stood where you see the replica today. The original was damaged in a 1527 riot (when a bench thrown from a palace window knocked its left arm off), but remained here for several centuries before being moved indoors for protection.

Step past the fake *David* through the front door into the Palazzo Vecchio's courtyard (free). This palace was Florence's symbol of civic power. You're surrounded by art for art's sake—a cherub frivolously marks the courtyard's center, and ornate stuccoes and frescoes

Piazza della Signoriai

decorate the walls and columns. Such luxury represented a big change 500 years ago. For more on this palace, see page 110.

▶ *Back outside, check out the statue-filled...*

Loggia dei Lanzi (a.k.a. Loggia della Signoria)

The loggia, once a forum for public debate, was perfect for a city that prided itself on its democratic traditions. But later, when the Medici figured that good art was more desirable than free speech, it was turned into an outdoor sculpture gallery. Notice the squirming Florentine themes—conquest, domination, rape, and decapitation. The statues lining the back are Roman originals brought back to Florence by a Medici when his villa in Rome was sold. Two statues in the front deserve a closer look.

The Rape of the Sabine Women (c. 1583), with its pulse-quickening rhythm of muscles, is from the restless Mannerist period, which followed the stately and confident Renaissance. The sculptor, Giambologna, proved his mastery of the medium by sculpting three entangled bodies from one piece of marble. The composition is best viewed from below and in front. The relief panel below shows a wider view of the terrible scene. (In the Accademia, you can see the plaster

Loggia dei Lanzi

The Rape of the Sabine Women, in the Loggia   *Perseus* recalls the classical world.

model of this statue that was used to guide Giambologna's workers in helping him create it.)

Benvenuto Cellini's **Perseus** (1545-1553), the loggia's most noteworthy piece, shows the Greek hero who decapitated the snake-headed Medusa. They say Medusa was so ugly she turned humans who looked at her to stone—though one of this book's authors thinks she's kinda cute.

► *Cross the square to Bartolomeo Ammanati's big fountain of Neptune that Florentines (including Michelangelo) consider a huge waste of marble—though one of this book's authors...*

The guy on the horse, to the left, is Cosimo I, one of the post-Renaissance Medici. Find the round marble plaque on the ground 10 steps in front of the fountain.

Savonarola Plaque

The Medici family was briefly thrown from power by an austere monk named Savonarola, who made Florence a constitutional republic. He organized huge rallies lit by roaring bonfires here on the square where he preached. While children sang hymns, the devout brought their rich "vanities" (such as paintings, musical instruments, and playing cards) and threw them into the flames.

But not everyone wanted a return to the medieval past.

Encouraged by the pope, the Florentines fought back and arrested Savonarola. For two days, they tortured him, trying unsuccessfully to persuade him to see their side of things. Finally, on the very spot where Savonarola's followers had built bonfires of vanities, the monk was burned. The plaque, engraved in Italian *("Qui dove…"),* reads, "Here, Girolamo Savonarola and his Dominican brothers were hanged and burned" in the year "MCCCCXCVIII" (1498).

▶ *Stay cool, we have 200 yards to go. Follow the gaze of the fake David into the courtyard of the two-tone horseshoe-shaped building.*

Uffizi Courtyard Statues

The top floor of this building, known as the *uffizi* (offices) during Medici days, is filled with the greatest collection of Florentine painting anywhere. It's one of Europe's top four or five art galleries (✪ see the Uffizi Gallery Tour chapter).

The Uffizi courtyard, filled with merchants and hustling young artists, is watched over by 19th-century statues of the great figures of the Renaissance. Tourists zero in on the visual accomplishments of the era, but let's pay tribute to the many other accomplishments of the Renaissance as well, as we wander through Florence's Hall of Fame.

▶ *Stroll down the left side of the courtyard from Palazzo Vecchio to the river, noticing the following greats.*

Lorenzo de' Medici (the Magnificent)—whose statue is tucked under the arcade, by an Uffizi doorway—was a great art patron and cunning power broker. Excelling in everything except modesty, he set the tone for the Renaissance.

Giotto, holding the plan to the city's bell tower—named for him—was the great pre-Renaissance artist whose paintings foretold the future of Italian art.

Donatello, the sculptor who served as a role model for Michelangelo, holds a hammer and chisel.

Alberti wrote a famous book, *On Painting,* which taught early Renaissance artists the mathematics of perspective.

Leonardo da Vinci was a scientist, sculptor, musician, engineer…and not a bad painter either.

Michelangelo ponders the universe and/or stifles a belch.

Dante, with the laurel-leaf crown and lyre of a poet, says, "I am the father of the Italian language." He was the first Italian to write a

Lorenzo the Magnificent outside the Uffizi

Machiavelli—the ends justify the means

popular work (*The Divine Comedy*) in non-Latin, using the Florentine dialect, which soon became "Italian" throughout the country.

The poet **Petrarch** wears laurel leaves from Greece, a robe from Rome, and a belt from Walmart.

Boccaccio wrote *The Decameron*, stories told to pass the time during the 1348 Black Death.

The devious-looking **Machiavelli** is hatching a plot—his book *The Prince* taught that the end justifies the means, paving the way for the slick-and-cunning "Machiavellian" politics of today.

Vespucci (in the corner) was an explorer who gave his first name, Amerigo, to a fledgling New World.

Galileo (in the other corner) holds the humble telescope he used to spot the moons of Jupiter.

▶ *Pause at the Arno River, overlooking...*

Ponte Vecchio

Before you is Ponte Vecchio (Old Bridge). A bridge has spanned this narrowest part of the Arno since Roman times. While Rome "fell," Florence really didn't, remaining a bustling trade center along the river. To get into the exclusive little park below (on the north bank), you'll need to join the Florence rowing club.

▶ *Finish your walk by hiking to the center of the bridge.*

A fine **bust** of the great goldsmith Cellini graces the central point of the bridge. This statue is a reminder that, in the 1500s, the

Spanning the Arno since 1345, Ponte Vecchio is barnacled with merchants' shops.

Medici booted out the bridge's butchers and tanners and installed the gold- and silversmiths who still tempt visitors to this day. Looking upstream and down, you have timeless views of the city. The neighborhood across the river, known as the Oltrarno, is more rustic and working-class.

Look up to notice the Vasari Corridor, the protected and elevated passageway that led the Medici from the Palazzo Vecchio through the Uffizi, across Ponte Vecchio, and up to the immense Pitti Palace, four blocks beyond the bridge. During World War II, the local German commander was instructed to blow up all of Florence's bridges to cover the Nazi retreat. But the art-loving commander blew up the others and left the Ponte Vecchio impassable but intact.

The Ponte Vecchio is a very romantic spot, especially in the evening. The sun sets behind the hills, and the bridges cast their reflection on the flat water. Street musicians play and lovers hold hands. The city of Florence—born in Roman times, flourishing in the medieval age, and blossoming in the Renaissance—is a vibrant city still, the cultural capital of Europe.

Accademia Tour: Michelangelo's *David*

Galleria dell'Accademia

One of Europe's great thrills is seeing Michelangelo's *David* in the flesh. Seventeen feet high, gleaming white, and exalted by a halo-like dome over his head, *David* rarely disappoints, even for those with high expectations. And the Accademia doesn't stop there. With a handful of other Michelangelo statues and a few other interesting sights, it makes for an uplifting visit that isn't overwhelming. *David* is a must-see on any visit to Florence, so plan for it.

...ENTATION

€12.50 (or €8 if there's no special exhibit), additional €4 fee for recommended reservation; covered by Firenze Card.

Hours: Tue-Sun 8:15-18:50, possibly Tue until 22:00 June-Sept, closed Mon.

Information: Reservation tel. 055-294-883, www.galleria-accademiafirenze.beniculturali.it.

Avoiding Lines: In peak season (April-Oct), it's smart to buy a Firenze Card or reserve ahead (see pages 165 and 166 for info on both options). Those with reservations or the Firenze Card line up at the entrance labeled *Reserved*. If you show up without a reservation or Firenze Card and there's a long line, the My Accademia Libreria reservation office (across the street from the exit) might have same-day reservations available (€4 fee). On off-season weekdays (Nov-March) before 8:30 or after 16:00, you can sometimes get in with no reservation and no lines. The museum is most crowded on Sun, Tue, before 18:00, and from 10:00 to 13:00.

Getting There: It's at Via Ricasoli 60, a 10-minute walk northeast of the Duomo.

Audioguides: €6 (€10/2 people). ∩ Download my free Accademia audio tour.

Length of This Tour: *David* and the *Prisoners* can be seen in 30 minutes. Allow another 30 minutes to explore the rest.

Security: You'll have to pass through a metal detector and put your bag through an X-ray (on crowded days, this can take up to 30 minutes). Leave pocketknives and corkscrews at your hotel. The museum has no bag-check service, and large backpacks are not allowed.

Cuisine Art: Gelateria Carabè, popular for its sumptuous *granite* (fresh-fruit Italian ices) is a block toward the Duomo, at Via Ricasoli 60 red. Picnickers can stock up at the Carrefour Express sandwich counter, a half-block north at Via Ricasoli 109 red. La Mescita Fiaschetteria serves inexpensive pasta and sandwiches, around the Accademia's south corner at Via degli Alfani 70 red.

Starring: Michelangelo's *David* and *Prisoners*.

Accademia Overview

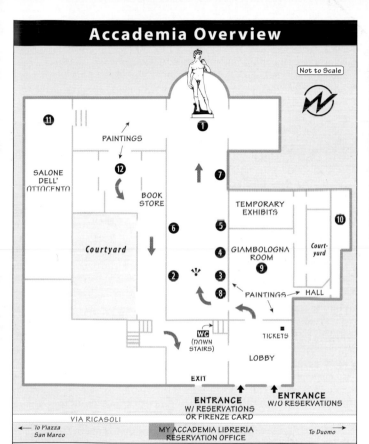

Not to Scale

PAINTINGS

① David

⑫

SALONE
DELL'
OTTOCENTO

⑪

BOOK
STORE

Courtyard

⑥

⑤

④

② ⚡ ③

⑧

TEMPORARY
EXHIBITS

GIAMBOLOGNA
ROOM
⑨

Courtyard

⑩

PAINTINGS

HALL

⑦

WC
(DOWN
STAIRS)

TICKETS

LOBBY

EXIT

ENTRANCE
W/ RESERVATIONS
OR FIRENZE CARD

ENTRANCE
W/O RESERVATIONS

VIA RICASOLI

← To Piazza
San Marco

MY ACCADEMIA LIBRERIA
RESERVATION OFFICE

To Duomo →

① David	⑦ Pietà
② Awakening Prisoner	⑧ Bust of Michelangelo
③ Young Prisoner	⑨ Rape of the Sabine Women
④ St. Matthew	⑩ Museum of Musical Instruments
⑤ Bearded Prisoner	⑪ Salone dell' Ottocento Statues
⑥ Atlas Prisoner	⑫ Florentine Paintings

THE TOUR BEGINS

▶ *From the entrance lobby, show your ticket, turn left, and look right down the long hall with* David *at the far end, under an illuminating circular skylight. Yes, you're really here. With* David *presiding at the "altar," the* Prisoners *lining the "nave," and hordes of "pilgrims" crowding in to look, you've arrived at Florence's "cathedral of humanism."*

Start with the ultimate...

David (1501-1504)

When you look into the eyes of Michelangelo's *David*, you're looking into the eyes of Renaissance Man. This 17-foot-tall symbol of divine victory over evil represents a new century and a whole new Renaissance outlook. This is the age of Columbus and classicism, Galileo and Gutenberg, Luther and Leonardo—of Florence and the Renaissance.

In 1501, Michelangelo Buonarroti, a 26-year-old Florentine, was commissioned to carve a large-scale work for the Duomo. He was given a block of marble that other sculptors had rejected as too tall, shallow, and flawed to be of any value. But Michelangelo picked up his hammer and chisel, knocked a knot off what became *David*'s heart, and started to work.

The figure comes from an Old Testament story. The Israelites, God's chosen people, are surrounded by barbarian warriors led by a brutish giant named Goliath. The giant challenges the Israelites to send out someone to fight him. Everyone is afraid except for one young shepherd boy—David. Armed only with a sling, which he's thrown over his shoulder, David gathers five smooth stones from the stream and faces Goliath.

The statue captures David as he's sizing up his enemy. He stands relaxed but alert, leaning on one leg in a classical pose known as *contrapposto*. In his powerful right hand, he fondles the handle of the sling, ready to fling a stone at the giant. His gaze is steady—searching with intense concentration, but also with extreme confidence. Michelangelo has caught the precise moment when David is saying to himself, "I can take this guy."

While some think that he's already slain the giant, the current director of the Accademia believes, as I do, that Michelangelo has

17-foot-tall, 12,000-pound symbol of Renaissance optimism, balanced atop a fragile right ankle

David, David, David, and David

Several Italian masters produced iconic sculptures of David—all of them different. Compare and contrast the artists' styles. How many ways can you slay a giant?

Donatello's *David* (1430, Bargello, Florence)
Donatello's *David* is young and graceful, casually gloating over the head of Goliath, almost Gothic in its elegance and smooth lines. While he has a similar weight-on-one-leg (*contrapposto*) stance as Michelangelo's later version, Donatello's *David* seems feminine rather than masculine. (For further description, see page 79 of the Bargello Tour chapter.)

Andrea del Verrocchio's *David* (c. 1470, Bargello, Florence)
Wearing a military skirt and armed with a small sword, Verrocchio's *David* is just a boy. The statue is only four feet tall—dwarfed by Michelangelo's monumental version. (For more, see page 80 of the Bargello Tour chapter.)

Michelangelo's *David* (1501-1504, Accademia, Florence)
Michelangelo's *David* is pure Renaissance: massive, heroic in size, and superhuman in strength and power. The tensed right hand, which grips a stone in readiness to hurl at Goliath, is

more powerful than any human hand. It's symbolic of divine strength. A model of perfection, Michelangelo's *David* is far larger and grander than we mere mortals. We know he'll win. Renaissance Man has arrived.

Gian Lorenzo Bernini's *David* (1623, Borghese Museum, Rome)

Flash forward more than a century. In this self-portrait, 25-year-old Bernini is ready to take on the world, slay the pretty-boy Davids of the Renaissance, and invent Baroque. Unlike Michelangelo's rational, cool, restrained *David,* Bernini's is a doer: passionate, engaged, dramatic. While Renaissance *David* is simple and unadorned—carrying only a sling—Baroque Dave is "cluttered" with

a braided sling, a hairy pouch, flowing cloth, and discarded armor. Bernini's *David,* with his tousled hair and set mouth, is one of us; the contest is less certain than with the other three *Davids.*

To sum up: Donatello's *David* represents the first inkling of the Renaissance; Verrocchio's is early Renaissance in miniature; Michelangelo's is textbook Renaissance; and Bernini's is the epitome of Baroque.

portrayed David facing the giant. (Unlike most depictions of David after the kill, this sculpture does not show the giant's severed head.)

David is a symbol of Renaissance optimism. He's no brute. He's a civilized, thinking individual who can grapple with and overcome problems. He needs no armor, only his God-given physical strength and wits. Look at his right hand, with the raised veins and strong, relaxed fingers—many complained that it was too big and overdeveloped. But this is the hand of a man with the strength of God. No mere boy could slay the giant. But David, powered by God, could...and did.

Originally, the statue was commissioned to stand atop the roof-line of the Duomo. But during the three years it took to sculpt, they decided instead to place it guarding the entrance of Town Hall—the Palazzo Vecchio. (If the relationship between *David*'s head and body seems a bit out of proportion, it's because Michelangelo designed it to be seen "correctly" from far below the rooftop of the church.)

The colossus was placed standing up in a cart and dragged across rollers from Michelangelo's workshop (behind the Duomo) to the Palazzo Vecchio, where it replaced a work by Donatello. There *David* stood—naked and outdoors—for 350 years. In the right light, you can see signs of weathering on his shoulders. Also, note the crack in *David*'s left arm where it was broken off during a 1527 riot near the Palazzo Vecchio. In 1873, to conserve the masterpiece, the statue was moved indoors and today resides under this wonderful Renaissance-style dome designed just for him, while a copy adorns the Palazzo Vecchio (see photo below).

Circle *David* and view him from various angles. From the front, he's confident, but a little less so when you gaze directly into his eyes. Around back, see his sling strap, buns of steel, and Renaissance mullet.

His oversized right hand, powered by God

David once guarded the Town Hall entrance.

Up close, you can see the blue-veined Carrara marble and a few cracks and stains. From the sides, Michelangelo's challenge becomes clear: to sculpt a figure from a block of marble other sculptors said was too tall and narrow to accommodate a human figure.

Renaissance Florentines could identify with *David*. Like him, they considered themselves God-blessed underdogs fighting their city-state rivals. In a deeper sense, they were civilized Renaissance people slaying the ugly giant of medieval superstition, pessimism, and oppression.

▶ *Hang around for a while. Eavesdrop on tour guides. The Plexiglas shields at the base of the statue are a reminder of an attack by a frustrated artist, who smashed the statue's feet in 1991.*

Lining the hall leading up to David are other statues by Michelangelo—his *Prisoners, St. Matthew,* and *Pictà. Start with the* Awakening Prisoner, *the statue at the end of the nave (farthest from David). He's on your left as you face David.*

The *Prisoners (Prigioni)*, c. 1516-1534

These unfinished figures seem to be fighting to free themselves from the stone. Michelangelo believed the sculptor was a tool of God, not creating but simply revealing the powerful and beautiful figures that God had encased in the marble. Michelangelo's job was to chip away the excess, to reveal. He needed to be in tune with God's will, and whenever the spirit came upon him, Michelangelo worked in a frenzy, without sleep, often for days on end.

The *Prisoners* give us a glimpse of this fitful process, showing the restless energy of someone possessed, struggling against the rock that binds him. Michelangelo himself fought to create the image he saw in his mind's eye. You can still see the grooves from the chisel, and you can picture Michelangelo hacking away in a cloud of dust. Unlike most sculptors, who built a model and then marked up their block of marble to know where to chip, Michelangelo always worked freehand, starting from the front and working back. These figures emerged from the stone (as his colleague Vasari put it) "as though surfacing from a pool of water."

The so-called **Awakening Prisoner** (the names are given by scholars, not Michelangelo) seems to be stretching after a long nap, still tangled in the "bedsheets" of uncarved rock. He's more block than statue.

More Michelangelo

If you're a fan of earth's greatest sculptor, don't leave Florence until there's a check next to each of these:

- **Bargello:** Several Michelangelo sculptures, including the *Bacchus* (pictured here; ✪ see the Bargello Tour chapter).
- **Duomo Museum:** Another moving pietà (see page 93).
- **Medici Chapels:** The *Night* and *Day* statues, plus others done for the Medici tomb, located at the Basilica of San Lorenzo (see page 114).
- **Laurentian Medici Library:** Michelangelo designed the entrance staircase and more, located at the Basilica of San Lorenzo (see page 114).
- **Palazzo Vecchio:** His *Victory* statue (see page 110).
- **Uffizi Gallery:** A rare Michelangelo painting (see page 66).
- **Casa Buonarroti:** Built on property Michelangelo once owned, at Via Ghibellina 70, containing some early works (see page 119).
- **Santa Croce Church:** Michelangelo's tomb (see page 118).
- **Santo Spirito Church:** Wooden crucifix thought to be by Michelangelo (see page 128).

On the right, the ***Young Prisoner*** is more finished. He buries his face in his forearm, while his other arm is chained behind him.

The *Prisoners* were designed for the never-completed tomb of Pope Julius II (who also commissioned the Sistine Chapel ceiling). Michelangelo may have abandoned them simply because the project itself petered out, or he may have deliberately left them unfinished. Having perhaps satisfied himself that he'd accomplished what he set out to do, and seeing no point in polishing them into their shiny, finished state, he went on to a new project.

Unfinished *Prisoner* fights to free himself.

Powerful pietà, possibly by Michelangelo

Walking up the nave toward *David*, you'll pass by Michelangelo's **St. Matthew** (1503), on the right. Though not one of the Prisoners series, he is also unfinished, perfectly illustrating Vasari's "surfacing" description

The next statue (also on the right), the **Bearded Prisoner,** is the most finished of the four, with all four limbs, a bushy face, and even a hint of daylight between his arm and body.

Across the nave on the left, the **Atlas Prisoner** carries the unfinished marble on his stooped shoulders, his head still encased in the block.

As you study the *Prisoners*, notice Michelangelo's love and understanding of the human body. His greatest days were spent sketching the muscular, tanned, and sweating bodies of the workers in the Carrara marble quarries. The prisoners' heads and faces are the least-developed part—they "speak" with their poses. Comparing the restless, claustrophobic *Prisoners* with the serene and confident *David* gives an idea of the sheer emotional range in Michelangelo's work.

Pietà

In the unfinished pietà (the threesome closest to *David*), the figures struggle to hold up the sagging body of Christ. Michelangelo (or, more likely, one of his followers) emphasizes the heaviness of Jesus' dead body, driving home the point that this divine being suffered a very human death. Christ's massive arm is almost the size of his bent and broken legs. By stretching his body—if he stood up, he'd be more than seven feet tall—the weight is exaggerated.

▶ *After getting your fill of Michelangelo, consider taking a spin around the rest of the Accademia. Michelangelo's statues are far and away the highlight here, but the rest of this small museum—housed in a former convent—has a few bonuses.*

Paintings
Browse the pleasant-but-underwhelming collection of paintings in the hall near *David* and the adjoining corridor; you'll be hard-pressed to find even one by a painter whose name you recognize. You'll find better art in the Giambologna Room near the exit (described later.)

Salone dell'Ottocento Statues
At the end of the hall to the left of *David* is a long room crammed with plaster statues and busts. These were the Academy art students' "final exams"—preparatory models for statues, many of which were later executed in marble. The black dots on the statues are sculptors' "points," guiding them on how deep to chisel. The Academy art school has been attached to the museum for centuries, and you may see the next Michelangelo wandering the streets nearby.

Bust of Michelangelo
At the end of the nave (farthest from *David*), a bronze bust depicts a craggy, wrinkled Michelangelo, age 88, by Daniele da Volterra. (Daniele, one of Michelangelo's colleagues and friends, is best known as the one who painted loincloths on the private parts of Michelangelo's nudes in the Sistine Chapel.) As a teenager, Michelangelo got his nose broken in a fight with a rival artist. Though Michelangelo went on to create great beauty, he was never classically handsome.

▶ *Enter the room near the museum entrance dominated by a large, squirming statue.*

Giambologna Room
This full-size plaster model of *Rape of the Sabine Women* (1582) guided Giambologna's assistants in completing the marble version in the Loggia dei Lanzi (on Piazza della Signoria, next to the Palazzo Vecchio, described on page 30). A Roman warrior tramples a fighter from the Sabine tribe and carries off the man's wife. Husband and wife exchange one final, anguished glance. Circle the statue and watch it spiral around its axis. Giambologna was clearly influenced (as a plaque

with photo points out) by Michelangelo's groundbreaking *Victory* in Palazzo Vecchio (1533-1534). Michelangelo's statue of a man triumphing over a fallen enemy introduced both the theme and the spiral-shaped pose that many artists imitated.

Browse the room clockwise (from the entrance) to locate minor paintings by artists you'll encounter elsewhere in Florence. Domenico Ghirlandaio's paintings of Renaissance Florence are behind the altar of the Church of Santa Maria Novella (see page 121). Francesco Grancacci assisted his childhood friend, Michelangelo, on the Sistine Ceiling. Benozzo Gozzoli decorated the personal chapel of the Medici in the Medici-Riccardi Palace (see page 116). Filippino Lippi is known for his frescoes in the Brancacci Chapel and Church of Santa Maria Novella. And Botticelli's *Birth of Venus* hangs in the Uffizi (see page 60).

▶ *From the Giambologna Room, head down a short hallway leading to a few rooms containing the...*

Museum of Musical Instruments

Between 1400 and 1700, Florence was one of Europe's most sophisticated cities, and the Medici rulers were trendsetters. Musicians like Scarlatti and Handel flocked to the court of Prince Ferdinando (1663-1713). You'll see late-Renaissance cellos, dulcimers, violins, woodwinds, and harpsichords. (Listen to some on the computer terminals.)

As you enter, look for the two group paintings that include the prince (he's second from the right in both paintings, with the yellow bowtie) hanging out with his musician friends. The gay prince played a mean harpsichord, and he helped pioneer new variations. In the adjoining room, you'll see several experimental keyboards, including some by Florence's keyboard pioneer, Bartolomeo Cristofori. The tall piano on display (from 1739) is considered by some to be the world's first upright piano.

▶ *Head one more time back up the nave to say goodbye to Dave; to exit, pass through the bookstore and into the open air for some sun, fresh air, peace, and quiet...aaaah.*

Uffizi Gallery Tour

Galleria degli Uffizi

In the Renaissance, Florentine artists rediscovered the beauty of the natural world. Medieval art had been symbolic, telling Bible stories. Realism didn't matter. But Renaissance people saw the beauty of God in nature and the human body. They used math and science to capture the natural world on canvas as realistically as possible.

The Uffizi Gallery (oo-FEET-zee) has the greatest overall collection anywhere of Italian painting. We'll trace the rise of realism and savor the optimistic spirit that marked the Renaissance. As Michelangelo wrote:

> *My eyes love things that are fair,*
> *and my soul for salvation cries.*
> *But neither will to Heaven rise*
> *unless the sight of Beauty lifts them there.*

€20 March-Oct (€10 if there's no special exhibit), €12 Nov-Feb (€6 if no special exhibit), additional €4 fee for recommended reservation; covered by Firenze Card.

Hours: Tue-Sun 8:15-18:50, closed Mon, last entry 45 minutes before closing.

Information: Reservation tel. 055-294-883, www.uffizi.it.

Renovation: The gallery is nearing the end of a major, multiyear overhaul. Pieces frequently move, and new rooms open, so expect changes.

Avoiding Lines: To skip the notoriously long ticket-buying lines (hours-long April-Oct), either get a Firenze Card or reserve ahead (for details on both, see pages 165 and 166). Without a Firenze Card or reservation, you can usually enter without major lines off-season after 16:00. During summer and on weekends, reserve a month or more in advance. The busiest days are Tuesday, Saturday, and Sunday.

Getting There: It's on the Arno River by the Palazzo Vecchio.

Getting In: There are several entrances (see map on page 52).

Door #1 (labeled *Reservation Entrance*), is for those with a Firenze Card or a reserved ticket already in hand. Get in the line for individuals—not groups—between door #1 and door #2. (To actually claim your reserved ticket, you must first go to door #3; see later.)

Door #2 is to buy same-day tickets (without a reservation). This door also sells Firenze Cards and same-day reservations (look for *Booking Service and Today* or *Advance Sale,* to the left of the same-day ticket-buying line).

Door #3 (labeled *Reservation Ticket Office*) is the first stop for those who've made reservations but need to pick up their tickets. Arrive 10 minutes before your appointed time. If you booked online and have already paid, you'll exchange your voucher for a ticket. If you (or your hotelier) booked by phone, show your confirmation number and pay. Once you have your ticket, walk across the courtyard and enter between Door #1 and #2.

Audioguides: €6 (€10/2 people; must leave ID). ∩ Download my free Uffizi Gallery audio tour.

Botticelli's *Venus*—for lovers of beauty

Crowded Uffizi entrance—plan ahead

Length of This Tour: Allow two hours.

Services: Baggage check is available in the entrance lobby; all backpacks and large bags must be checked. A WC, post office, and extensive book/gift shop are in the entrance/exit hall on the ground floor. The Uffizi guidebook makes a nice souvenir. Once in the gallery, there are no WCs until the end of our tour, on the staircase leading down from the café.

Cuisine Art: The café at the top end of the gallery has an outdoor terrace with stunning views of the Palazzo Vecchio and the Duomo's dome. They serve pricey sandwiches, salads, and desserts, but a €5 cappuccino with that view is one of Europe's great treats.

Starring: Botticelli, Venus, Raphael, Giotto, Titian, Leonardo, and Michelangelo.

THE TOUR BEGINS

▸ *Walk up the four long flights of the monumental staircase to the top floor. (Those with limited mobility can take the elevator.) Past the ticket taker, get oriented.*

Overview

The Uffizi is U shaped, running around the courtyard. This left wing contains Florentine paintings from medieval to Renaissance times. The right wing (which you can see across the courtyard) has a rare painting by Michelangelo, and a view café terrace. A short hallway with sculpture connects the two wings. We'll concentrate on the Uffizi's forte, the Florentine section, then get a taste of the art that followed.

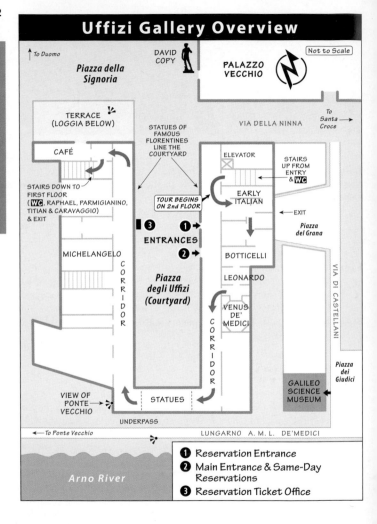

Uffizi Gallery Overview

Not to Scale

To Duomo

DAVID COPY

PALAZZO VECCHIO

Piazza della Signoria

TERRACE (LOGGIA BELOW)

VIA DELLA NINNA

To Santa Croce

CAFÉ

STATUES OF FAMOUS FLORENTINES LINE THE COURTYARD

ELEVATOR

STAIRS UP FROM ENTRY & WC

STAIRS DOWN TO FIRST FLOOR (WC, RAPHAEL, PARMIGIANINO, TITIAN & CARAVAGGIO) & EXIT

TOUR BEGINS ON 2nd FLOOR

EARLY ITALIAN

EXIT

Piazza del Grana

❸ ENTRANCES ❶

MICHELANGELO

CORRIDOR

❷

BOTTICELLI

LEONARDO

Piazza degli Uffizi (Courtyard)

VENUS DE' MEDICI

CORRIDOR

VIA DI CASTELLANI

Piazza dei Giudici

VIEW OF PONTE VECCHIO

STATUES

GALILEO SCIENCE MUSEUM

UNDERPASS

To Ponte Vecchio

LUNGARNO A. M. L. DE'MEDICI

Arno River

❶ Reservation Entrance
❷ Main Entrance & Same-Day Reservations
❸ Reservation Ticket Office

▶ *Head up the long hallway, enter the first door on the left, and come face-to-face Giotto's giant Virgin Mary on a throne.*

Medieval—When Art Was as Flat as the World (1200-1400)

Duccio, Cimabue, and Giotto, a Trio of Madonnas with Child

Mary and Baby Jesus sit on a throne in a golden never-never land symbolizing heaven. It's as if medieval Christians couldn't imagine holy people inhabiting our dreary material world. It took Renaissance painters to bring Mary down to earth and give her human realism. For the Florentines, "realism" meant "three-dimensional."

The three similar-looking Madonna-and-Bambinos in this room—all painted within a few decades of each other, in about the year 1300—show baby steps in the march to realism. **Duccio**'s piece (on the left as you face Giotto) is the most medieval and two-dimensional. There's no background. The angels are just stacked one on top of the other, floating in the golden atmosphere. Mary's throne is crudely drawn—the left side is at a three-quarter angle while the right is practically straight on. Mary herself is a wispy cardboard-cutout figure seemingly floating just above the throne.

Duccio's *Madonna*—a cardboard cutout; Cimabue—more substantial; Giotto—massive Mary on 3-D throne

On the opposite wall, the work of **Cimabue**—mixing the iconic Byzantine style with budding Italian realism—is an improvement. The large throne creates an illusion of depth. Mary's foot actually sticks out over the lip of the throne. Still, the angels are stacked totem-pole-style, serving as heavenly bookends.

Giotto employs realism to make his theological points. He creates a space and fills it. Like a set designer, he builds a three-dimensional "stage"—the canopied throne—then peoples it with real beings. The throne has angels in front, prophets behind, and a canopy over the top, clearly defining its three dimensions. The steps up to the throne lead from our space to Mary's, making the scene an extension of our world. But the real triumph here is Mary herself—big and monumental, like a Roman statue. Beneath her robe, she has a real live body, with knees and breasts that stick out at us. This three-dimensionality was revolutionary in its day, a taste of the Renaissance a century before it began.

Giotto was one of the first "famous" artists. In the Middle Ages, artists were mostly unglamorous craftsmen, like carpenters or cable-TV repairmen. They cranked out generic art. But Giotto was recognized as a genius, a unique individual. He died in a plague that devastated Florence. If there had been no plague, would the Renaissance have started 100 years earlier?

▶ *Enter Room 3, to the left as you face Giotto.*

Simone Martini, *Annunciation*

Simone Martini (c. 1284-1344) boils things down to the basic figures needed to get the message across: (1) The angel appears to sternly tell (2) Mary that she'll be the mother of Jesus. In the center is (3) a vase of lilies, a symbol of purity. Above is (4) the Holy Spirit as a dove about to descend on her. If the symbols aren't enough to get the message across, Simone Martini has spelled it right out for us in Latin: *"Ave Gratia Plena..."* or, "Hail, favored one, the Lord is with you." Mary doesn't exactly look pleased as punch.

This is not a three-dimensional work. The point was not to re-create reality but to teach religion, especially to the illiterate masses. This isn't a beautiful Mary or even a real Mary. She's a generic woman without distinctive features. We know she's pure—not from her face, but because of the halo and symbolic flowers. Before the Renaissance, artists didn't care about the beauty of individual people.

Simone Martini's *Annunciation* has medieval features you'll see in many of the paintings in the next few rooms: (1) religious subject, (2) gold background, (3) two-dimensionality, and (4) meticulous detail.

▶ *Pass through Rooms 4-6, full of golden altarpieces. Exiting Rooms 5-6, hang a U-turn left into Room 7.*

Gentile da Fabriano, *Adoration of the Magi*

Look at the incredible detail of the Three Kings' costumes, the fine horses, and the cow in the cave. Fabriano (c. 1370-1427) filled the canvas from top to bottom with realistic details—but it's far from realistic. While the Magi worship Jesus in the foreground, their return trip home dangles over their heads in the "background."

This is a textbook example of the International Gothic style popular with Europe's aristocrats in the early 1400s: well-dressed, elegant people in a colorful, design-oriented setting. The religious subject is just an excuse to paint secular luxuries such as jewelry and clothes made of silk brocade. And the scene's background and foreground are compressed together to create an overall design that's pleasing to the eye. Such exquisite detail work raises the question: Was Renaissance three-dimensionality truly an improvement over Gothic, or simply a different style?

Early Renaissance (mid-1400s)

▶ *Enter Room 8. Look straight ahead, to a painting of Mary with her hands folded and Baby Jesus being lifted up by playful angel boys.*

Fra Filippo Lippi, *Madonna and Child with Two Angels*

Mentally compare this Mary with the generic female in Simone

Annunciation—saints in golden Neverland

Adoration—exquisite detail, cramped 3-D

Martini's Annunciation. We don't need the wispy halo over her head to tell us she's holy—she radiates sweetness and light from her divine face. Heavenly beauty is expressed by a physically beautiful woman.

Fra (Brother) Lippi (1406-1469), an orphan raised as a monk, lived a less-than-monkish life. He lived with a nun who bore him two children. He spent his entire life searching for the perfect Virgin. Through his studio passed Florence's prettiest girls, many of whom decorate the walls here in this room.

Lippi painted idealized beauty, but his models were real flesh-and-blood human beings. You could look through all the thousands of paintings from the Middle Ages and not find anything so human as the mischievous face of one of Lippi's little angel boys.

▶ *Nearby—either here in Room 8 or in the following Room 9—find a free-standing double portrait.*

Piero della Francesca, Federico da Montefeltro and Battista Sforza

In medieval times, only saints and angels were worthy of being painted. In the humanistic Renaissance, however, even nonreligious folk like this husband and wife by Francesca (c. 1412-1492) had their features preserved for posterity. Usually the man would have appeared on the left, with his wife at the right. But Federico's right side was definitely not his best—he lost his right eye and part of his nose in a tournament. Renaissance artists discovered the beauty in ordinary people and painted them, literally, warts and all.

▶ *In Room 9, find the glass case with two tiny works by Pollaiolo.*

Warts-and-all celebration of a real man

Beautiful *Madonna* radiates holiness.

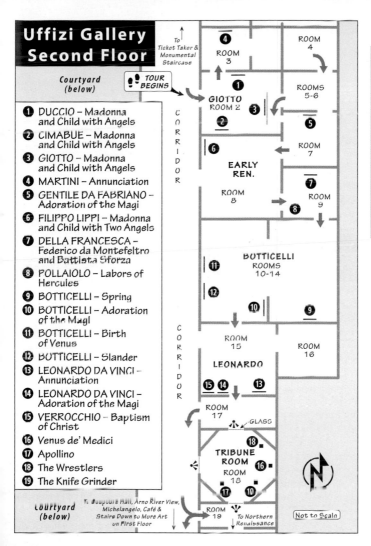

Uffizi Gallery Second Floor

Courtyard (below)

TOUR BEGINS

❶ DUCCIO – Madonna and Child with Angels
❷ CIMABUE – Madonna and Child with Angels
❸ GIOTTO – Madonna and Child with Angels
❹ MARTINI – Annunciation
❺ GENTILE DA FABRIANO – Adoration of the Magi
❻ FILIPPO LIPPI – Madonna and Child with Two Angels
❼ DELLA FRANCESCA – Federico da Montefeltro and Battista Sforza
❽ POLLAIOLO – Labors of Hercules
❾ BOTTICELLI – Spring
❿ BOTTICELLI – Adoration of the Magi
⓫ BOTTICELLI – Birth of Venus
⓬ BOTTICELLI – Slander
⓭ LEONARDO DA VINCI – Annunciation
⓮ LEONARDO DA VINCI – Adoration of the Magi
⓯ VERROCCHIO – Baptism of Christ
⓰ Venus de' Medici
⓱ Apollino
⓲ The Wrestlers
⓳ The Knife Grinder

To Ticket Taker & Monumental Staircase

ROOM 3
ROOM 4
ROOMS 5-6
GIOTTO ROOM 2
ROOM 7
EARLY REN.
ROOM 8
ROOM 9
BOTTICELLI ROOMS 10-14
ROOM 15
ROOM 16
LEONARDO
ROOM 17
GLASS
TRIBUNE ROOM
ROOM 18
ROOM 19

CORRIDOR

Courtyard (below)

To Sculpture Hall, Arno River View, Michelangelo, Café & Stairs Down to More Art on First Floor

To Northern Renaissance

Not to Scale

Pollaiolo dissected corpses to learn how to depict realistic musculature in extreme poses.

Antonio del Pollaiolo, *Labors of Hercules*

Hercules gets a workout in two small panels showing the human form at odd angles. The poses are the wildest imaginable, to show how each muscle twists and tightens. While Uccello worked on perspective, Pollaiolo (c. 1431-1498) studied anatomy. In medieval times, dissection of corpses was a sin and a crime (the two were the same then). Dissecting was a desecration of the human body, the temple of God. But Pollaiolo was willing to sell his soul to the devil for artistic knowledge. He dissected.

There's something funny about this room that I can't put my finger on...I've got it—no Madonnas. Not one. (No, that's not a Madonna; she's a Virtue.)

We've seen how Early Renaissance artists worked to conquer reality. Now let's see the fruits of their work, the flowering of Florence's Renaissance.

▶ *Enter the large space (Rooms 10-14) where works by Botticelli are displayed.*

The Renaissance Blossoms (1450-1500)

Florence in 1450 was in a Firenz-y of activity. There was a can-do spirit of optimism in the air, led by prosperous merchants and bankers and a strong middle class. The government was reasonably democratic, and Florentines saw themselves as citizens of a strong republic—like ancient Rome. Their civic pride showed in the public monuments and artworks they built. Man was leaving the protection of the church to stand on his own two feet.

Lorenzo de' Medici, head of the powerful Medici family, epitomized this new humanistic spirit. Strong, decisive, handsome, poetic, athletic, sensitive, charismatic, intelligent, brave, clean, and reverent, Lorenzo was a true Renaissance man, deserving of the nickname he went by—the Magnificent. He gathered Florence's best and brightest around him for evening wine and discussions of great ideas. One of this circle was the painter Botticelli.

Sandro Botticelli, *Spring*

It's springtime in a citrus grove. The winds of spring blow in (Mr. Blue, at right), causing the woman on the right to sprout flowers from her lips as she morphs into Flora, or Spring—who walks by, spreading flowers from her dress. At the left are Mercury and the Three Graces,

Botticelli's *Primavera* captures the springtime of the Renaissance, showing gods on earth.

dancing a delicate maypole dance. The Graces may be symbolic of the three forms of love—of beauty, love of people, and sexual love, suggested by the raised intertwined fingers. (They forgot love of peanut butter on toast.) In the center stands Venus, the Greek goddess of love. Above her flies a blindfolded Cupid, happily shooting his arrows of love without worrying whom they'll hit.

Here is the Renaissance in its first bloom, its "springtime" of innocence. Madonna is out, Venus is in. Adam and Eve hiding their nakedness are out, glorious flesh is in. This is a return to the pre-Christian pagan world of classical Greece, where things of the flesh are not sinful. But this is certainly no orgy—just fresh-faced innocence and playfulness.

Botticelli (1445-1510) emphasizes pristine beauty over gritty realism. The lines of the bodies, especially of the Graces in their see-through nighties, have pleasing, S-like curves. The faces are idealized but have real human features. There's a look of thoughtfulness and even melancholy in the faces—as though everyone knows that the innocence of spring will not last forever.

▶ *You may (or may not) find the following painting nearby, giving a glimpse into the world of the Medici.*

Botticelli, *Adoration of the Magi*

Here's the rat pack of confident young Florentines who reveled in the optimistic pagan spirit—even in a religious scene. Botticelli included himself among the adorers, at the far right, looking vain in the yellow robe. Lorenzo is the Magnificent-looking guy at the far left.

▶ *Now approach the room's most famous painting, thronged by admirers.*

Botticelli, *Birth of Venus*

According to myth, Venus was born from the foam of a wave. Still only half awake, this fragile, newborn beauty floats ashore on a clamshell, blown by the winds, where her maid waits to dress her. The pose is the same S-curve of classical statues (as we'll soon see). Botticelli's pastel colors make the world itself seem fresh and newly born.

This is the purest expression of Renaissance beauty. Venus' naked body is not sensual, but innocent. Botticelli thought that physical beauty was a way of appreciating God. Remember Michelangelo's poem: Souls will never ascend to heaven "...unless the sight of Beauty lifts them there."

The Greek Goddess of Love slowly awakens after a thousand years of medieval darkness.

Botticelli finds God in the details—Venus' windblown hair, her translucent skin, the maid's braided hair, the slight ripple of the wind god's abs, and the flowers tumbling in the slowest of slow motions, suspended like musical notes, caught at the peak of their brief life.

Mr. and Mrs. Wind intertwine—notice her hands clasped around his body. Their hair, wings, and robes mingle like the wind. But what happened to those splayed toes?

▶ *"Venus on the Half-Shell" (as many tourists call this) is one of the masterpieces of Western art. Take some time with it. Then find a small canvas nearby depicting a more turbulent scene.*

Botticelli, *Slander,* a.k.a. *Calumny of Apelles*

The spring of Florence's Renaissance had to end. Lorenzo died young. The economy faltered. Into town rode the monk Savonarola, preaching medieval hellfire and damnation for those who embraced the "pagan" Renaissance spirit. "Down, down with all gold and decoration," he roared. "Down where the body is food for the worms." He presided over huge bonfires, where the people threw in their fine clothes, jewelry, pagan books...and paintings.

Slander spells the end of the Florentine Renaissance. The architectural setting is classic Brunelleschi, but look what's taking place

Botticelli's *Slander*—chaos reigns   Leonardo's *Annunciation*—underlying order

beneath those stately arches. These aren't proud Renaissance men and women but a ragtag, medieval-looking bunch, a Court of Thieves in an abandoned hall of justice. The accusations fly, and everyone is condemned. The naked man pleads for mercy, but the hooded black figure, a symbol of his execution, turns away. The figure of Truth (naked Truth)—straight out of *The Birth of Venus*—looks up to heaven as if to ask, "What has happened to us?" The classical statues in their niches look on in disbelief.

Botticelli listened to Savonarola. He burned some of his own paintings and changed his tune. The last works of his life were darker, more somber, and pessimistic about humanity.

The 19th-century German poet Heinrich Heine said, "When they start by burning books, they'll end by burning people." After four short years of power, Savonarola was burned in 1498 on his own bonfire in Piazza della Signoria, but by then the city was in shambles. The first flowering of the Renaissance was over.

▶ *Enter the next room (#15), and find another* Annunciation *scene, by one of Florence's brightest lights.*

Leonardo da Vinci, *Annunciation*

A scientist, architect, engineer, musician, and painter, Leonardo da Vinci (1452-1519) was a true Renaissance man. He worked at his own pace rather than to please an employer, so he often left works unfinished. The two paintings in this room aren't his best, but even a lesser Leonardo is enough to put a museum on the map, and they're definitely worth a look.

In the *Annunciation,* the angel Gabriel has walked up to Mary, and now kneels on one knee like an ambassador, saluting her. See how relaxed his other hand is, draped over his knee. Mary, who's been reading, looks up with a gesture of surprise and curiosity.

Leonardo constructs a beautifully landscaped "stage" and puts his characters in it. Look at the bricks on the right wall. If you extended lines from them, the lines would all converge at the center of the painting, the distant blue mountain. Same with the edge of the sarcophagus and the railing. This subtle touch creates a subconscious feeling of balance, order, and spaciousness in the viewer.

Think back to Simone Martini's *Annunciation* to realize how much more natural, relaxed, and realistic Leonardo's version is. He's taken a miraculous event—an angel appearing out of the blue—and presented it in a very human way.

Leonardo da Vinci, *Adoration of the Magi*

Leonardo's human insight is even more apparent here, in this unfinished work (it may be under restoration during your visit). The poor kings are amazed at the Christ child—even afraid of him. They scurry around like chimps around a fire. This work is as agitated as the *Annunciation* is calm, giving us an idea of Leonardo's range. Leonardo was pioneering a new era of painting, showing not just the outer features but the inner personality.

Nearby hangs the *Baptism of Christ* by Andrea del Verrocchio, Leonardo's teacher. Leonardo painted the angel on the far left when he was only a teenager. Legend has it that when Verrocchio saw that some kid had painted an angel better than he ever would...he hung up his brush for good.

Florence saw the first blossoming of the Renaissance. But when the cultural climate turned chilly, artists flew south to warmer climes. The Renaissance shifted to Rome.

▶ *Proceed past the Leonardo into the small hallway. Straight ahead is a doorway (with a glass barrier) to the Tribuna (a.k.a. Room 18). Gazing inside, you'll see the famous* Venus de' Medici *statue.*

Tribune Room

If the Renaissance was the foundation of the modern world, the foundation of the Renaissance was classical sculpture. Sculptors, painters, and poets alike turned for inspiration to these ancient Greek and Roman works as the epitome of balance, 3-D perspective, human anatomy, and beauty.

Venus de' Medici, first century B.C.

Is this pose familiar? Botticelli's *Birth of Venus* has the same position of the arms, the same S-curved body, and the same lifting of the right leg. A copy of this statue stood in Lorenzo the Magnificent's garden, where Botticelli used to hang out. This one is a Roman copy of the lost original by the great Greek sculptor Praxiteles. Balanced, harmonious, and serene, the statue embodies the attributes of Greece's "Golden Age," when balance was admired in every aspect of life.

Perhaps more than any other work of art, this statue (*Venere dei Medici*) has been the epitome of both ideal beauty and sexuality. In the 18th and 19th centuries, sex was "dirty," so the sex drive of cultured aristocrats was channeled into a love of pure beauty. Wealthy sons and daughters of Europe's aristocrats made the pilgrimage to the Uffizi to complete their classical education...where they swooned in ecstasy before the cold beauty of this goddess of love.

Louis XIV had a bronze copy made. Napoleon stole her away to Paris for himself. And in Philadelphia in the 1800s, a copy had to be kept under lock and key to prevent the innocent from catching the Venere-al disease. At first, it may be difficult for us to appreciate such passionate love of art, but if any generation knows the power of sex to sell something—be it art or underarm deodorant—it's ours.

The Other Statues, first-second century A.D.

Venus's male counterpart is leaning on a tree trunk, facing Venus. *Apollino* (a.k.a. "Venus with a Penis") was also carved by that ancient Greek master of smooth, cool lines: Praxiteles.

The other works are later Greek (Hellenistic), when quiet balance was replaced by violent motion and emotion. *The Wrestlers,* to the left of Venus, is a study in anatomy and twisted limbs—like Pollaiolo's paintings a thousand years later.

The drama of *The Knife Grinder* to the right of Venus stems from the offstage action—he's sharpening the knife to flay a man alive.

This fine room was a showroom, or a "cabinet of wonders," back when this building still functioned as the Medici offices. Filled with family portraits, it's a holistic statement that symbolically links the Medici family with the four basic elements: air (weathervane in the lantern), water (inlaid mother of pearl in the dome), fire (red wall), and earth (inlaid stone floor).

▶ *Exit into the main hallway. Breathe. Sit. Admire the ceiling. Look out the window. See you in five. Back already? Now continue down the hall, where a nude statue welcomes you to the...*

Sculpture Hall

A hundred years ago, no one even looked at Botticelli—they came to the Uffizi to see the sculpture collection. And today, these 2,000-year-old Roman copies of 2,500-year-old Greek originals are hardly noticed...but they should be. Only a few are displayed here now.

The most impressive is the male nude, **Doriforo** ("spear carrier"), a Roman copy of the Greek original by Polykleitos (located in the middle of the hallway, where it turns right).

The purple statue in the center of the hall—headless and limbless—is a **female wolf** (*lupa*, c. A.D. 120) done in porphyry stone. This was the animal that raised Rome's legendary founders and became the city's symbol. Renaissance Florentines marveled at the ancient Romans' ability to create such lifelike, three-dimensional works. They learned to reproduce them in stone...and then learned to paint them on a two-dimensional surface.

▶ *Gaze out the windows from the hall for a...*

View of the Arno and Ponte Vecchio

This is my favorite view of the river and Ponte Vecchio. You can also see the red-tiled roof of the Vasari Corridor, the "secret" passage connecting the Palazzo Vecchio, Uffizi, Ponte Vecchio, and Pitti Palace on the other side of the river—a half-mile in all. This was a private walkway, wallpapered in great art, for the Medici family's commute from home to work.

As you appreciate the view, remember that it's this sort of pleasure that Renaissance painters wanted you to get from their paintings. For them, a canvas was a window you looked through to see the wide world. Their paintings re-create natural perspective: Distant objects (such as bridges) are smaller, dimmer, and higher up the "canvas," while closer objects are bigger, clearer, and lower.

We're headed down the home stretch now. If your little U-feetsies are killing you, and it feels like torture, remind yourself that it's a pleasant torture and smile...like the statue next to you.

▶ *Round the bend and start down the far hallway. About 40 yards down, at the fourth doorway, turn left into Room 35 and head for the round painting opposite the entry.*

Michelangelo Room

Michelangelo Buonarroti, *Holy Family*, a.k.a. *Doni Tondo*

This is the only completed easel painting by the greatest sculptor in history. Florentine painters were sculptors with brushes; this shows it. Instead of a painting, it's more like three clusters of statues with some clothes painted on.

The main subject is the holy family—Mary, Joseph, and Baby Jesus—and in the background are two groups of nudes looking like classical statues. The background represents the old pagan world, while Jesus in the foreground is the new age of Christianity. The figure of young John the Baptist at right is the link between the two.

This is a "peasant" Mary, with a plain face and sunburned arms. Michelangelo (1475-1564) shows her from a very unflattering angle—we're looking up her nostrils. But Michelangelo himself was an ugly man, and he was among the first artists to recognize the beauty in everyday people.

Michelangelo was a Florentine—in fact, he was like an adopted son of the Medici, who recognized his talent—but much of his greatest work was done in Rome as part of the pope's face-lift of the city. We can see here some of the techniques he used on the Sistine Chapel ceiling that revolutionized painting—monumental figures; dramatic angles (looking up Mary's nose); accentuated, rippling muscles; and bright, clashing colors (all the more apparent since both this work and the Sistine Chapel ceiling have been recently cleaned). These elements added a dramatic tension that was lacking in the graceful work of Leonardo and Botticelli.

Michelangelo painted this for his friend Agnolo Doni for 70 ducats. (Michelangelo designed, but didn't carve, the elaborate frame.) When the painting was delivered, Doni tried to talk Michelangelo down to 40. Proud Michelangelo took the painting away and would not sell it until the man finally agreed to pay double...140 ducats.

Also on display in the room is the hard-to-miss statue of *Sleeping Ariadne.* The third-century work was much copied, and Michelangelo was inspired by it. (Hmm. Does Mary in the Doni Tondo have a few touches of Ariadne? The twisting pose, the position of the arms, and the heavily wrinkled robe?)

▶ *Return to the hallway and continue to the end—past the special*

Michelangelo's *Holy Family*—earthy

Raphael's *Madonna*—graceful and balanced

*exhibits and rooms where masterpieces from closed rooms are tempo-
rarily displayed.*

Rest of the Top Floor

Laocoön (16th-Century Copy)

At the far end of the hall is a copy of the dramatic ancient Greek statue
of *Laocoön* (the original is at the Vatican Museums). It depicts the moment when this priest of Troy is overcome by snakes, and he realizes
his people are doomed. ("Snakes? Why did it have to be snakes?") One
of the most famous statues of antiquity, it was discovered in 1506—just
in time to inspire Renaissance greats like Michelangelo. After seeing
Laocoön, Michelangelo began creating figures with more restless motion and tragic emotion. *Laocoön*'s anguished face may exude tragedy, but right now Mr. Laocoon seems to be saying, "Time for a coffee
break." Just past him is a fine café and an open-air terrace where you
can enjoy a truly aesthetic experience...

Little Capuchin Monk (Cappuccino)

This drinkable art form, born in Italy, is now enjoyed all over the world. It's called the "Little Capuchin Monk" because the coffee's frothy, light- and dark-brown foam looks like the two-toned cowls of the Capuchin order. Sip it on the terrace in the shadow of the towering Palazzo Vecchio, and be glad we live in an age where you don't need to be a Medici to enjoy all this fine art. Salute.

▶ *When you're ready to move on, go down the staircase near the café, to the first floor. On your way down, you'll pass the WC. Once on the first floor, we'll be making our way through dozens of rooms with a lot more art. Breeze through quickly, making a few key stops along the way.*

First Floor—More Art on the Way to the Exit

At the bottom of the staircase, turning right, you enter Room 56, a long red-walled room lined with the kind of **ancient statues** that inspired Renaissance painters. Continue through more rooms to Room 65, with **portraits by Bronzino** of Duke Cosimo I de' Medici, his wife, Eleonora, their cute bird-holding son, and their daughters.

▶ *Stop in Room 66 for...*

Raphael, *Madonna of the Goldfinch*

Raphael (Raffaello Sanzio, 1483-1520) brings Mary and bambino down from heaven and into the real world of trees, water, and sky. He gives Baby Jesus (right) and John the Baptist a realistic, human playfulness. It's a tender scene painted with warm colors and a hazy background that matches the golden skin of the children.

Raphael perfected his craft in Florence, following the graceful style of Leonardo. In typical Leonardo fashion, this group of Mary, John the Baptist, and Jesus is arranged in the shape of a pyramid, with Mary's head at the peak.

The two halves of the painting balance perfectly. Draw a line down the middle, through Mary's nose and down through her knee. John the Baptist on the left is balanced by Jesus on the right. Even the trees in the background balance each other, left and right. These things aren't immediately noticeable, but they help create the subconscious feelings of balance and order that reinforce the atmosphere of maternal security in this domestic scene—pure Renaissance.

▶ *On the wall to the left is...*

Six Degrees of Leo X

This sophisticated, luxury-loving pope was at the center of an international Renaissance world that spread across Europe. He crossed paths with many of the Renaissance men of his generation. Based on the theory that any two people are linked by only "six degrees of separation," let's link Leo X with the actor Kevin Bacon:

- Leo X's father was Lorenzo the Magnificent, patron of Botticelli and Leonardo.
- When Leo X was age 13, his family took in 13-year-old Michelangelo.
- Michelangelo inspired Raphael, who was later hired by Leo X.
- Raphael exchanged masterpieces with fellow genius Albrecht Dürer, who was personally converted by Martin Luther (who was friends with Lucas Cranach), who was excommunicated by...Leo X.

- Leo X was portrayed in the movie *The Agony and the Ecstasy*, which starred Charlton Heston, who was in *Two-Minute Warning* with J. A. Preston, who was in *A Few Good Men* with...Kevin Bacon.

Raphael, *Pope Leo X with Cardinals Giulio de' Medici and Luigi de' Rossi*

Raphael was called to Rome at the same time as Michelangelo, working next door in the Vatican apartments while Michelangelo painted the Sistine Chapel ceiling. Raphael peeked in from time to time, learning from Michelangelo's monumental, dramatic figures, and his later work is grittier and more realistic than the idealized, graceful, and "Leonardoesque" Madonna

Pope Leo X is big, like a Michelangelo statue. And Raphael captures some of the seamier side of Vatican life in the cardinals' eyes—shrewd, suspicious, and somewhat cynical. With Raphael, the photographic realism pursued by painters since Giotto was finally achieved.

The Florentine Renaissance ended in 1520 with the death of Raphael. Raphael (see his self-portrait nearby) is considered both the culmination and conclusion of the Renaissance. The realism, balance, and humanism we associate with the Renaissance are all found in Raphael's work. He combined the grace of Leonardo with the power of Michelangelo. With his death, the High Renaissance ended as well.

▶ *A few rooms farther along, you reach Room 74, with a tall painting.*

Parmigianino, *Madonna with the Long Neck*

Mannerists such as Parmigianino (1503-1540) tried to go beyond realism, exaggerating it for effect. Using brighter colors and twisting poses, they created scenes more elegant and more exciting than real life.

By stretching the neck of his Madonna, Parmigianino (like the cheese) gives her an unnatural, swanlike beauty. She has the same pose and position of hands as Botticelli's *Venus* and the *Venus de' Medici*. Her body forms an arcing S-curve—down her neck as far as her elbow, then back the other way along Jesus' body to her knee, then down to her foot. Baby Jesus seems to be blissfully gliding down this slippery slide of sheer beauty.

▶ *Continue on to long Room 83, with a number of works by Titian.*

Titian, *Venus of Urbino*

Compare this *Venus* with Botticelli's newly hatched *Venus,* and you get a good idea of the difference between the Florentine and Venetian Renaissances. Botticelli's was pure, innocent, and otherworldly. Titian's should have a staple in her belly button. This isn't a Venus, it's a centerfold—with no purpose but to please the eye (and other organs). While Botticelli's allegorical *Venus* is a message, this is a massage. The bed is used.

Titian (c. 1490-1576) and his fellow Venetians took the pagan spirit pioneered in Florence and carried it to its logical hedonistic conclusion. Using bright, rich colors, they captured the luxurious life of happy-go-lucky Venice.

While other artists may have balanced their compositions with a figure on the left and one on the right, Titian balances his painting in a different way—with color. The canvas is split down the middle by the curtain. The left half is dark, the right half is lighter. The two halves are connected by a diagonal slash of luminous gold—the nude woman. The girl in the background is trying to find her some clothes.

Titian's *Venus*—a Renaissance centerfold—is warm and sensual, with a come-hither look.

In the Uffizi, we've seen many images of female beauty: from ancient goddesses to medieval Madonnas, from Parmigianino's cheesy slippery-slide to Michelangelo's peasant Mary, from Botticelli's pristine nymphs to Titian's sensuous centerfold. Their physical beauty expresses different aspects of the human spirit.

► *Our tour is n-n-n-nearly over. Turn left through a long connecting hallway, then again into still more rooms. It's worth pausing in Room 90, with works by Caravaggio, including the shocking ultrarealism of* Sacrifice of Isaac *and macabre head of* Medusa, *painted on a ceremonial shield.*

When you're ready to leave, the exit takes you back down to the WCs/bookstore/post office, and the way out to the street. You'll pop out behind the Uffizi, a block up from the river and very near the Galileo Science Museum and the Bargello (sculpture museum). Stepping back into the real world after your Uffizi experience, you may see it with new eyes.

Bargello Tour

The Renaissance began with sculpture. The great Florentine painters were "sculptors with brushes." You can see the birth of this revolution of 3-D in the Bargello (bar-JEL-oh), which boasts the best collection of Florentine sculpture.

You'll meet Donatello's *David,* a sly little boy who slew a giant. The museum has the original contest panels for the Baptistery doors, the event that kicked off the Renaissance. And there are several Michelangelo statues—less-famous works that show off different aspects of his varied style.

A small, uncrowded museum and a pleasant break from the intensity of the rest of Florence, the Bargello shows off 150 years of great statues, spanning the history of Florence's heyday. And it's all set in a rustic palazzo with a medieval atmosphere.

ORIENTATION

Cost: €8, cash only, covered by Firenze Card.

Hours: Tue-Sat 8:15-17:00, later for special exhibits, until 13:50 Nov-March; also open these times on the second and fourth Mon and first, third, and fifth Sun of each month. You can reserve an entrance time, but it's unnecessary.

Information: Tel. 055-238-8606, www.bargellomusei.beniculturali.it.

Getting There: Via del Proconsolo 4, a three-minute walk northeast of the Uffizi.

Getting In: You must pass through a metal detector, and bags go through an X-ray machine before you enter.

Audioguide: ∩ Download my free Bargello audio tour.

Length of This Tour: Allow one hour. If your time is limited, be sure to see the Michelangelo statues on the ground floor and the Donatello *David* statues on the first.

Cuisine Art: Inexpensive bars and cafés are in nearby streets.

Starring: Michelangelo, Donatello, Brunelleschi, Ghiberti, and four different *David*s.

THE TOUR BEGINS

Courtyard

▶ *Buy your ticket and take a seat in the courtyard.*

The Bargello, built in 1255, was Florence's original Town Hall and also served as a police station *(bargello),* and later a prison. The heavy fortifications tell us that keeping the peace in medieval Florence had its occupational hazards.

This cool and peaceful courtyard is at the center of the three-story rectangular building. The best statues are found in two rooms—one on the ground floor at the foot of the outdoor staircase, and another one flight up, directly above. We'll proceed from Michelangelo to Donatello to Verrocchio.

But first, meander around this courtyard and get a feel for sculpture in general and the medium of stone in particular. Sculpture is a much more robust art form than painting. Think of just the engineering problems of the sculpting process: quarrying and cutting the stone, transporting the block to the artist's studio, all the hours of chiseling away chips, then the painstaking process of sanding the final product by hand. A sculptor must be strong enough to gouge into the stone, but delicate enough to groove out the smallest details. Think of Michelangelo's approach to sculpting: He wasn't creating a figure—he was liberating it from the rock that surrounded it.

The Renaissance was centered on humanism—and sculpture is the perfect medium in which to express it. It shows the human form, standing alone, independent of church, state, or society, ready to fulfill its potential.

Finally, a viewing tip. Every sculpture has an invisible "frame" around it—the stone block it was cut from. Visualizing this frame helps you find the center of the composition.

Ground Floor

▶ Head into the room at the foot of the courtyard's grand staircase, turn left, and be greeted by a tall, marble party animal.

Michelangelo, *Bacchus*, c. 1497

Bacchus, the god of wine and revelry, raises another cup to his lips, while his little companion goes straight for the grapes.

Maybe Michelangelo had a sense of humor after all. Mentally compare this tipsy Greek god of wine with his sturdy, sober *David*, begun a few years later. Raucous Bacchus isn't nearly so muscular, so monumental...or so sure on his feet. Hope he's not driving. The pose, the smooth muscles, the beer belly, and the swaying hips look more like Donatello's boyish *David (upstairs)*.

This was Michelangelo's first major commission. He often vacillated between showing man as strong and noble, or as weak and perverse. This isn't the nobility of the classical world, but the decadent side of orgies and indulgence.

▶ *Just beyond* Bacchus *is...*

Michelangelo, *Brutus*, 1540

Another example of the influence of Donatello is this so-ugly-he's-beautiful bust by Michelangelo. His rough intensity gives him the look of a man who has succeeded against all odds, a dignified and heroic quality that would be missing if he were too pretty.

The subject is Brutus, the Roman who, for the love of liberty, murdered his friend and dictator, Julius Caesar (*"Et tu...?"*). Michelangelo could understand this man's dilemma. He himself was torn between his love of the democratic tradition of Florence and loyalty to his friends the Medici, who had become dictators.

So he gives us two sides of a political assassin. The right profile (the front view) is heroic. But the hidden side, with the drooping mouth and squinting eye, makes him more cunning, sneering, and ominous.

▶ *Nearby is...*

Another side to Michelangelo besides *David: Bacchus* (left) is debauched, while *Brutus* broods

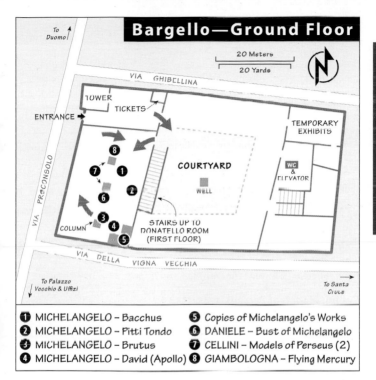

Bargello—Ground Floor

To Duomo

20 Meters
20 Yards

VIA GHIBELLINA

TOWER

TICKETS

ENTRANCE →

VIA PROCONSOLO

TEMPORARY EXHIBITS

COURTYARD

WC & ELEVATOR

WELL

8
7 **1**
6 **2**
3 **4**
COLUMN **5**

STAIRS UP TO DONATELLO ROOM (FIRST FLOOR)

VIA DELLA VIGNA VECCHIA

To Palazzo Vecchio & Uffizi

To Santa Croce

1 MICHELANGELO – Bacchus
2 MICHELANGELO – Pitti Tondo
3 MICHELANGELO – Brutus
4 MICHELANGELO – David (Apollo)
5 Copies of Michelangelo's Works
6 DANIELE – Bust of Michelangelo
7 CELLINI – Models of Perseus (2)
8 GIAMBOLOGNA – Flying Mercury

Michelangelo, *David*, a.k.a. *Apollo*, 1530-1532

This restless, twisting man is either David or Apollo. (Is he reaching for a sling or a quiver?) Demure (and left unfinished), this statue is light years away from Michelangelo's famous *David* in the Accademia (1501-1504), which is so much larger than life in every way. We'll see three more *David*s upstairs. As you check out each one, compare and contrast the artists' styles.

In the glass cases in the corner are **small-scale copies** of some of Michelangelo's most famous works. In the center of the room, against a square column, look for a dark-bronze **bust of Michelangelo** by his fellow sculptor Daniele da Volterra, capturing his broken nose and

Donatello (1386-1466)

Donatello was the first great Renaissance genius, a model for Michelangelo and others. He mastered realism, creating the first truly lifelike statues of people since ancient times. Dontello turned out highly personal work. Unlike the ancient Greeks—but like the ancient Romans—he often sculpted real people, not idealized versions of pretty gods and goddesses. Some of these people are downright ugly. In the true spirit of Renaissance humanism, Donatello appreciated the beauty of flesh-and-blood human beings.

Donatello's personality was also a model for later artists. He was moody and irascible, purposely setting himself apart from others in order to concentrate on his sculpting. He developed the role of the "mad genius" that Michelangelo would later perfect.

brooding nature. (You may recognize this bust from the Accademia, which has a copy.)

▶ Doubling back toward the entrance, you'll find...

Cellini, *Models of Perseus,* 1545-1554
The life-size statue of Perseus slaying Medusa, located in the open-air loggia next to the Palazzo Vecchio, is cast bronze. Benvenuto Cellini started with these smaller models (one in wax, one in bronze) to master the difficult process of producing the first bronze statue of its kind in the Renaissance. Next to the statue, note the exquisite pedestal with four fine bronzes—built to support Cellini's statue of Perseus.

▶ Take three steps toward the door to find...

Giambologna, *Flying Mercury,* before 1580
Catch this statue while you can—he's in a hurry to deliver those flowers. Despite all the bustle and motion, Mercury has a solid Renaissance core: the line of balance that runs straight up the center, from toes to hip to fingertip. He's caught in midstride. His top half leans forward, counterbalanced by his right leg in back, while the center of gravity rests firmly at the hipbone. Down at the toes, notice the cupid practicing for the circus.

Bargello—First Floor

To Duomo

20 Meters
20 Yards

VIA GHIBELLINA

TOWER

CHAPEL

VIA PROCONSOLO

⓫ ⓬ ⓭
⓮
⓾
DONATELLO
ROOM
❾

COURTYARD

ELEVATOR

STAIRS UP FROM
GROUND FLOOR

UPPER
LOGGIA

STAIRS UP TO
SECOND FLOOR

VIA DELLA VIGNA VECCHIA

To Palazzo
Vecchio & Uffizi

To Santa →
Croce

❾ DONATELLO – David (c. 1408)
⓾ VERROCCHIO – David (c. 1469)
⓫ DONATELLO – David (c. 1440)
⓬ DESIDERIO – Niccolò da Uzzano

⓭ DONATELLO – St. George
⓮ GHIBERTI & BRUNELLESCHI – The Sacrifice of Isaac (2 versions)

▶ To see the roots of Florence's Renaissance, climb the courtyard staircase to the next floor up and turn right into the large Donatello room.

First Floor

▶ Entering the room, cross to the middle of the far wall, and check out the first of three Davids in this room (the marble one wearing the long skirt)

Donatello, *David*, c. 1408

This is young Donatello's first take on the popular subject of David slaying Goliath. His dainty pose makes him a little unsteady on his

Verrocchio's *David*—small but confident

Donatello's *David*—coy, sensuous, and nude

feet. He's dressed like a medieval knight—fully clothed but showing some leg through the slit skirt. The generic face and blank, vacant eyes give him the look not of a real man but of an anonymous decoration on a church facade. At age 22, Donatello still had one foot in the old Gothic world. To tell the story of David, Donatello plants a huge rock right in the middle of Goliath's forehead.

▶ *Nearby, find a smaller, black-metal statue. It's the same subject, of David, but by a different artist.*

Andrea del Verrocchio, *David*, c. 1466-1469

Verrocchio (1435-1488) is best known as the teacher of Leonardo da

Vinci, but he was also the premier sculptor of the generation between Donatello and Michelangelo. Verrocchio's bronze *David* is definitely the shepherd "boy" described in the Bible. (Some have speculated that the statue was modeled on Verrocchio's young, handsome, curly-haired apprentice, Leonardo da Vinci.) David leans on one leg, not with a firm, commanding stance but a nimble one (especially notice-able from behind). Compare the smug smile of the victor with Goliath's "Oh, have I got a headache" expression.

▶ *Finally, near the corner, is...*

Donatello, *David*, c. 1440

He's naked. Donatello sees David as a teenage boy wearing only a hel-met, boots, and sword. The smooth skinned warrior sways gracefully, poking his sword playfully at the severed head of the giant Goliath. His *contrapposto* stance is similar to Michelangelo's *David*, resting his weight on one leg in the classical style, but it gives him a feminine rather than masculine look. Gazing into his coy eyes and at his bulging belly is a very different experience from confronting Michelangelo's older and sturdier Renaissance Man.

This *David* paved the way for Michelangelo's. Europe hadn't seen a freestanding male nude like this in a thousand years. In the Middle Ages, the human body was considered a dirty thing, a symbol of man's weakness, something to be covered up in shame. The church prohib-ited exhibitions of nudity like this one and certainly would never deco-rate a church with it. But in the Renaissance, a new class of rich and powerful merchants appeared, and they bought art for personal enjoy-ment. Reading Plato's *Symposium*, they saw the ideal of Beauty in the form of a young man. This particular statue stood in the palace of the Medici (today's Medici-Riccardi Palace)...where Michelangelo, practi-cally an adopted son, grew up admiring it.

▶ *Along the wall behind the last* David *is...*

Donatello (or Desiderio da Settignano), *Niccolò da Uzzano*, after 1450

Not an emperor, not a king, not a pope, saint, or prince, this is one of Florence's leading businessmen, in a toga, portrayed in the style of an ancient Roman bust. In the 1400s, when Florence was inventing the Renaissance that all Europe would soon follow, there was an optimis-tic spirit of democracy that gloried in everyday people. Donatello (or his student) portrayed this man as he was—with wrinkles, a quizzical look, and bags under his eyes.

▶ *In the niche at the end of the room stands...*

Donatello, *St. George,* c. 1417

The proud warrior has both feet planted firmly on the ground and stands on the edge of his niche looking out alertly. He tenses his powerful right hand as he prepares to attack. George, the Christian slayer of dragons, was just the sort of righteous warrior proud Renaissance Florentines could rally around in their struggles with nearby cities. Nearly a century later, Michelangelo's *David* replaced George as the unofficial symbol of Florence, but David was clearly inspired by George's relaxed intensity and determination. (This is the original statue; a copy stands in its original niche at Orsanmichele Church— see page 25.)

The relief panel below shows George doing what he's been pondering. To his right, the sketchy arches and trees create the illusion of a distant landscape. Donatello, who apprenticed in Ghiberti's studio, is credited with teaching his master how to create 3-D illusions like this.

An ordinary businessman shown heroically

Donatello's *St. George* inspired Florentines.

► *On the wall next to* George, *you'll find some bronze relief panels. Don't look at the labels just yet.*

Ghiberti and Brunelleschi, Baptistery Door Competition Entries, 1401

Some would say these two different relief panels (pictured on the next page) represent the first works of the Renaissance. These two versions of *The Sacrifice of Isaac* were finalists in a contest held in 1401 to decide who would create the bronze doors of the Baptistery. The contest sparked citywide excitement, which evolved into the Renaissance spirit. Lorenzo Ghiberti won and later did the doors known as the Gates of Paradise. Filippo Brunelleschi lost—fortunately for us—freeing him to design the dome of the cathedral (or Duomo)

Both artists catch the crucial moment when Abraham, obeying God's orders, prepares to slaughter and burn his only son as a sacrifice. At the last moment—after Abraham has passed this test of faith—an angel of God appears to stop the bloodshed.

Let's look at the composition of the two panels: One is integrated and cohesive (yet dynamic), while the other is a balanced knickknack shelf of segments. Human drama: One has bodies and faces that speak. The boy's body is a fine classical nude in itself, so real and vulnerable. Abraham's face is intense and ready to follow God's will. Perspective: An angel zooms in from out of nowhere to save the boy in the nick of time.

Is one panel clearly better than the other? You be the judge. Pictured on the next page are the two finalists for the Baptistery door competition—Ghiberti's and Brunelleschi's. Which do you like best?

It was obviously a tough call, but Ghiberti's was chosen, perhaps because his goldsmith training made him better suited for the technical work. (Ghiberti used the lost-wax technique to cast his bronze panels. This was far cheaper than Brunelleschi's panels, which were molded with solid bronze. Economics may have entered into the decision-making process.)

Whatever the reason, Ghiberti got the gig, and that started a historic chain of events: Ghiberti went on to make the famous Baptistery doors, the ones so popular with tourists. Meanwhile, Brunelleschi was free to build his awe-inspiring dome. And Donatello graduated from Ghiberti's workshop to revolutionize sculpture. All three of these

Ghiberti's, on the left, won.

artists inspired Michelangelo, who built on their work and spread the Renaissance all across Europe. And it all started with these panels.

The Rest of the Bargello

Our tour is done. But, there's much more to see from the dynamic Renaissance. At the other end of this room are painted, glazed porcelains by the masterful Della Robbia family. Elsewhere on this floor, you can browse jewelry, ivories, and traditional Tuscan majolica ceramics. There's even an upper floor, with medallions, armor, colorful terra-cotta, and models of famous statues.

From swords to statues, from *Brutus* to Brunelleschi, from *David* to *David* to *David* to *David*—the Bargello's collection of civilized artifacts makes it clear that Florence was the birthplace of the Renaissance.

Duomo Museum Tour

Museo dell'Opera del Duomo

The recently remodeled Duomo Museum offers one of Italy's great artistic experiences. Five centuries ago, Italian artists decorated Florence's Duomo, Baptistery, and Campanile with amazing art. Now these treasures are gathered inside, protected from the elements, in a marvelous museum.

Brunelleschi's dome, Ghiberti's bronze doors, and Donatello's statues: These creations define the 1400s (the Quattrocento) in Florence, when the city blossomed and classical arts were reborn.

Copies of the doors and statues now decorate the exteriors of the cathedral, Baptistery, and Campanile, while the original sculptured masterpieces of the complex are now restored and thoughtfully displayed here. The museum also has two powerful statues by Florence's powerhouse sculptors—Donatello's Mary Magdalene and Michelangelo's *Pietà*, intended as his sculptural epitaph.

ORIENTATION

Cost: €15 combo-ticket covers all Duomo sights, valid 48 hours, covered by Firenze Card.

Hours: Daily 9:00-20:00, closed first Tue of every month. This is one of the few museums in Florence that's open every Monday.

Information: Tel. 055-230-2885, www.museumflorence.com.

Getting There: The museum is across from the Duomo on the east side (the far end from the Baptistery), at Via del Proconsolo 9.

Tours: A free app for the Duomo Museum is available from iTunes and Google Play.

Length of This Tour: Allow 1.5 hours. With limited time, focus on Ghiberti's doors, Michelangelo's *Pietà,* Donatello's sculptures, and the pair of finely carved choir lofts (cantorie).

Services: All backpacks must be checked, regardless of size; purses and messenger bags are OK. Ticket machines in the lobby allow you to make Duomo dome-climb reservations—see page 107. Several WCs are available inside.

Starring: Brunelleschi, Ghiberti, Donatello, and Michelangelo.

THE TOUR BEGINS

Ground Floor

The museum presents the 2,000-year history of Florence's Duomo, Baptistery, and Campanile.

▶ *Scan your ticket, and pass the hall lined with names of the many great artists and architects who helped build the Duomo over the centuries. Enter Room 4, with a large...*

Model of the Duomo's Medieval Facade

The model shows the church facade circa 1500, the era of Michelangelo. Notice that only the lower third of the facade is faced with marble and statues. The rest was only bare brick. Church construction began in 1296, but after an initial burst of energy, petered out. The facade was meant to be a glorious showcase of great statues set into niches. Get close to the model and find a few: There's Mary-and-Babe over the central doorway. Above and to her left is a pope with a ridiculously tall hat. And below Mary are four seated evangelists.

▶ *Now let's see those actual statues, and more from the medieval facade. Continue into the large hall, Room 6, dubbed the...*

Hall of Paradise (Sala del Paradiso)

This room re-creates that lower third of the facade we saw on the model: One long wall showing the facade niches and arches, and the opposite exhibiting the facade and Baptistery doors. Both buildings were a showcase of the greatest art of Florence from roughly 1300 to 1600. In this room, the original statues, doors, and reliefs face each other as they once did on the buildings they were designed for.

Start with the Duomo. The Duomo began life in early medieval times as a humble church overshadowed by the more prestigious Baptistery. By the 1200s, the church wasn't big enough to contain the exuberant spirit of a city growing rich from the wool trade and banking. So in 1296, Florence set out to rebuild it, intending to make the finest church of the age.

Arnolfo di Cambio, the architect, began the construction and designed the facade. Arnolfo envisioned a three-story facade of pointed arches and white, pink, and green marble, studded with statues, and gleaming with gold mosaics. In fact, it might have looked much like the Neo-Gothic version on the church today. For the next two

Duomo Museum—Ground Floor

STAIRS UP TO FIRST FLOOR

Room 9

Not to Scale

Room 7

Rm 12

Room 8

Room 10

Room 4

STAIRS & ELEV.

SHOP

STAIRS

Room 6

Room 5

TEMPORARY EXHIBITIONS

WC

TICKETS

COURTYARD

ELEV.

DUOMO FACADE

HALL OF PARADISE

BAPTISTRY FACADE

TOUR BEGINS

COAT ROOM

CAFE

ENTRANCE

To Duomo Entrance

Piazza del Duomo

To Opera del Duomo Studio

❶ Model of the Duomo's Medieval Facade

❷ ARNOLFO – Madonna with the Glass Eyes

❸ DONATELLO – St. John the Evangelist

❹ ARNOLFO – Pope Boniface VIII

❺ GHIBERTI – "Gates of Paradise" Doors

❻ GHIBERTI – North Doors

❼ PISANO – South Doors

❽ DONATELLO – Mary Magdalene

❾ Relics

❿ MICHELANGELO – Pietà

centuries, great sculptors contributed to the facade. But it was never completed. Only the bottom third was faced with marble—the upper part remained bare brick.

Still, what they did complete is very impressive. It was a showcase for the city's top sculptors. In its niches were late Gothic and early Renaissance statues—some of the best of the age.

▶ *Let's get a closer look at some of the statues. Find the seated* Madonna and Child, *flanked by saints. The original is on ground level (so tourists can see it better), while a copy stands above, showing her original location on the facade.*

Madonna over the door

Donatello's *St. John*—power and gravitas

Arnolfo di Cambio, Madonna with the Glass Eyes (Madonna dagli Occhi di Vetro), c. 1300

This is the central figure over the cathedral's doorway. The building was dedicated to Mary—starry-eyed over the birth of Baby Jesus. She sits, crowned like a chess-set queen, framed with a dazzling mosaic halo. To the right is St. Zenobius, Florence's first bishop during Roman times, whose raised hand consecrates the formerly pagan ground as Christian.

▶ *Flanking the Madonna in the four big niches are the Four Evangelists (left to right: Matthew, Luke, John, and Mark). Focus on...*

Donatello, St. John the Evangelist, c. 1409

John sits gazing at a distant horizon, his tall head rising high above his massive body. This visionary foresees a new age...and the coming Renaissance. With its expressive face, this work is a hundred years ahead of its time.

At 22 years old, Donatello (c. 1386-1466) sculpted this work just before becoming a celebrity for his inspiring statue of St. George (original in the Bargello, copy on the exterior of the Orsanmichele Church). Donatello ("Little Donato"), like most early Renaissance artists, was a blue-collar worker, raised as a workshop apprentice among knuckle-dragging musclemen. He proudly combined physical skill with technical know-how to create beauty (Art + Science = Renaissance Beauty). His statues are thinkers with big hands who can put theory into practice.

▶ *At the far left of the room is the original statue of the pope with the tall hat. The copy sits high up on the facade, just left of center.*

Arnolfo di Cambio, *Pope Boniface VIII*

Despised by Dante for his meddling in politics, Pope Boniface paid 3,000 florins to get his image in a box seat high on the facade. While he looks stretched out when viewed at ground level, Arnolfo portrayed him out of proportion intentionally. His XXL shirt size looks right when he's up above and viewed from street level.

▶ *Facing the facade of the church, as they did in the Middle Ages, are the famous doors of the Baptistery. Here's your chance to study the original panels of those famous bronze doors.*

Ghiberti's Gates of Paradise

The Renaissance began in 1401 with a citywide competition to build new doors for the Baptistery. Lorenzo Ghiberti (c. 1378-1455) won the job and built the doors for the north side of the building. Everyone loved them, so he was then hired to make another set of doors for the east entrance, facing the Duomo. These bronze "Gates of Paradise" revolutionized the way Renaissance people saw the world around them.

Ghiberti, the illegitimate son of a goldsmith, labored all his working life (more than 50 years) on the two sets of Baptistery doors. Their execution was a major manufacturing job, requiring a large workshop of artists and artisans for each stage of the process: making the door frames that hold the panels, designing and forming models of the panels in wax (to cast them in bronze); gilding the panels (by painting them with powdered gold dissolved in mercury, then heating the panels until the mercury burned off, leaving the gold); polishing and mounting the panels; installing the doors...and signing paychecks for everyone along the way. Ghiberti was as much businessman as artist.

Each panel is bronze with a layer of gold on top. They tell several stories in one frame using perspective and realism as never before. Ghiberti poured his energy and creativity into these panels. That's him in the center of the door frame, atop the second row of panels—the head on the left with the shiny male-pattern baldness. His son (and assistant) is to his right.

These original 10 panels were moved from the Baptistery to the museum to better preserve them. (Copies adorn the Baptistery itself.) Now they are under glass to protect against natural light and preserved in nitrogen to guard them from oxygen and humidity.

Moving from left to right and top to bottom, here are the Old Testament stories depicted in each panel:

Adam and Eve: God creates Adam, Eve, the snake, the apple, and original sin, then expels the humans.

Cain and Abel: Cain and Abel tend sheep, till the soil, and make a sacrifice, then Cain kills Abel and talks to God.

Noah: Noah and sons emerge from the ark (shown as a pyramid) after the flood, then Noah makes a sacrifice and gets drunk.

Abraham and Isaac: An angel prevents the sacrifice of Isaac.

Jacob and Esau: Isaac's son Jacob buys and deceives his way into the birthright of his elder brother, Esau.

Joseph and Benjamin: After his brothers sell him into slavery in Egypt, Joseph recognizes them when they visit and frames Benjamin as a thief.

Moses: Onlookers exult as Moses receives the Tablets of the Law from God.

Joshua: Joshua leads the chosen people into the Promised Land in celebration as the walls of Jericho fall.

David: The young hero conquers the giant Goliath.

Solomon and the Queen of Sheba: After traveling to Jerusalem with a great retinue and many gifts, a queen meets a king.

Armed with new rules of perspective, Ghiberti rendered reality with a mathematical precision revolutionary for the time. To understand how these advances made visual space feel more real than ever before, study the following three panels:

The space created by the arches in the Jacob and Esau panel is as interesting as the scenes themselves. At the center is the so-called vanishing point on the distant horizon, where all the arches and floor

Ghiberti's Baptistery door panels: *Creation of Adam and Eve* (left) and *Cain and Abel*—a mountainside murder

Joseph and Benjamin—a temple in the round

Solomon and Sheba—all eyes go toward them

tiles converge. Those closest to us, at the bottom of the panel, are big and clearly defined. Distant figures are smaller, fuzzier, and higher up. Ghiberti has placed us as part of this casual crowd of holy people—some with their backs to us—milling around an arcade.

In the Joseph and Benjamin panel, notice how, with just the depth of a thumbnail, Ghiberti creates a temple in the round that's inhabited by workers. This round temple wowed the Florentines. Suddenly the world acquired a whole new dimension—depth.

The receding arches stretch into infinity in the Solomon and the Queen of Sheba panel, giving the airy feeling that we can see forever. All of the arches and steps converge at the center of the panel, where the two monarchs meet, uniting their respective peoples. Ghiberti's subject was likely influenced by the warm ecumenical breeze blowing through Florence in 1439, as religious leaders convened here in an attempt to reunite the eastern (centered on Constantinople) and western (Rome) realms of Christendom.

▶ *Exit the Hall of Paradise and pass through Room 7 and into Room 8 to find an evocative wooden statue of an emaciated woman.*

Donatello, *Mary Magdalene (Santa Maria Maddalena)*, c. 1455

Carved from white poplar and originally painted with realistic colors, this statue is a Renaissance work of intense devotion. Mary Magdalene—the prostitute rescued from the streets by Jesus—folds her hands in humble prayer. Her once-beautiful face and body have been scarred by fasting, repentance, and the fires of her own remorse. The matted hair sticks to her face; veins and tendons line the emaciated arms and neck. The rippling hair suggests emotional turmoil within. But from her hollow, tired eyes, you see a deep need for repentance, not idealized, praying to be forgiven. The rendering of her feet, arms, chest, and face make clear that Donatello understood the body and had a passion to show it realistically.

▶ *Duck into Room 9 to see a collection of...*

Relics

Impressive, shiny vessels contain the mortal remains of saints, which helped connect the devout to the long-dead. Among the reliquaries, you'll find a slender Gothic pillar in the shape of a steeple. It holds John the Baptist's finger. This severed index finger of the beheaded prophet is the most revered relic of all the holy body parts in this museum. Also notice the large gem-studded gold cross that holds a purported fragment of the True Cross. Study the exquisite containers, which illustrate the importance of holy relics in medieval times.

▶ *Backtrack into Room 8, pass Mary, and continue to Room 10 and meet the maestro...*

Michelangelo, *Pietà*, 1547-1555

Three mourners tend the broken body of the crucified Christ. We see Mary, his mother (the shadowy figure on our right); Mary Magdalene (on the left, polished up by a pupil); and Nicodemus, the converted Pharisee, whose face is that of Michelangelo himself. The polished body of Christ stands out from the unfinished background. Michelangelo (as Nicodemus), who spent a lifetime bringing statues to life by "freeing" them from the stone, looks down at what could be his final creation, the once-perfect body of Renaissance Man that is now twisted, disfigured, and dead.

A pietà—by definition—shows Mary mourning her dead son, taken off the cross. The theological point: Jesus died to save us. The artist's goal: to show him dead. Michelangelo made the dead weight of Jesus' body profound—you feel the downward pull. In fact, he sculpted Jesus in a Z-shape, taller than he probably was to accentuate the weight of his dead body. Notice also the intimacy of mother and son—Mary was with her son at his birth and at his death...struggling to support him.

The aging Michelangelo (1475-1564) designed his own tomb, with this as the centerpiece. He was depressed by old age, and the grim reality that by sculpting this statue, he was writing his own obituary. As it was done on his own dime, it's fair to consider this an introspective and very personal work.

Michelangelo's late *Pietá,* intended for his own tomb, includes his hooded self-portrait.

▸ *Before leaving, look at the doorway to the left of the Pietà and find the tiny plaque indicating the level of the water during the terrible flooding of the Arno on November 4, 1966. The flood damaged many of these works, then in their original setting inside the Duomo. After being restored, they were moved here to be kept in a more secure environment.*

Now, exit through the doorway on the right to the staircase. Go up the steps and, at the landing, turn right into the...

First Floor

Gallery of the Campanile Decorations (Galleria del Campanile)

The museum has the original 16 statues (by several sculptors) from the bell tower's third story, where copies stand today.

▸ *Start with the panels immediately on the left and work your way down the row. We'll focus on the statues later.*

Andrea Pisano (and Others), Campanile Panels, c. 1334-1359

These 28 hexagonal and 28 diamond-shaped, blue-glazed panels decorated the Campanile, seven per side (where copies stand today). The original design scheme may have been Giotto's, but his successor, Andrea Pisano, and assistants executed the work.

The panels celebrate technology, showing workers, inventors, and thinkers. Allegorically, they depict humanity's long march to "civilization"—a blend of art and science, brain and brawn. But realistically, they're snapshots of that industrious generation that helped Florence bounce back ferociously from the Black Death of 1348.

The lower, hexagonal panels (reading left to right) show God starting the chain of creation by inventing (1) man and (2) woman, and so on. Skipping ahead a dozen panels—just after the last door—find the famed invention of sculpture, as an artist chisels a figure to life.

The upper diamond-shaped panels, made of marble on blue majolica (tin-glazed pottery tinged blue with cobalt sulfate), add religion (sacraments and virtues) to the march-of-civilization equation.

▸ *Now turn your attention to the other side of the room, the line of 16 statues that adorned the bell tower. Notice that the statues differ in quality, as they were made by different sculptors from different*

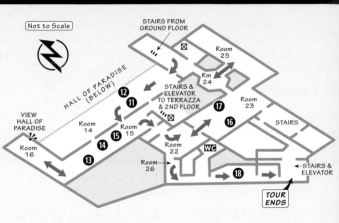

Duomo Museum—First Floor

PISANO (& Others) – Campanile Panels
DONATELLO – Jeremiah & Habakkuk
Tools & Scaffolding
BRUNELLESCHI – Models of the Cupola & Lantern
Brunelleschi's Death Mask
DELLA ROBBIA – Cantoria
DONATELLO – Cantoria
Evolution of the Facade

generations. The sixth and seventh statues in line, in particular, stand out. These are the prophets Jeremiah and Habakkuk by the early Renaissance master Donatello.

Donatello, *Jeremiah (Geremia, 1427-1436)* and *Habakkuk (Abacuc, 1434-1436)*

Donatello did several statues of the prophets, plus some others with collaborators. In the process, he developed the Renaissance style that Michelangelo would later perfect—powerful, expressive, and ultra-realistic, sculpted in an "unfinished" style by an artist known for experimentation and his prickly, brooding personality.

Start with Jeremiah. Watching Jerusalem burn in the distance, the prophet reflects on why the Israelites wouldn't listen when he warned them that the Babylonian kings would conquer the city. He purses his lips bitterly, and his downturned mouth is accentuated by his plunging neck muscle and sagging shoulders. The folds in the clothes are very deep, evoking the anger, sorrow, and disgust that Jeremiah feels but cannot share, as it is too late. Movement, realism, and human drama were Donatello's great contributions to sculpture.

Next, find the bald prophet Habakkuk. Donatello's signature piece shows us the wiry man beneath the heavy mantle of a prophet. From the deep furrows of his rumpled cloak emerges a bare arm with well-defined tendons and that powerful right hand. His long, muscled neck leads to a bald head (the Italians call the statue *Lo Zuccone*, meaning "pumpkin head"). This is realism.

The ugly face, with several days' growth of beard, crossed eyes, and tongue-tied mouth, looks crazed. This is no confident Charlton Heston prophet, but a man who's spent too much time alone, fasting in the wilderness, searching for his calling, and who now returns to babble his vision on a street corner.

Donatello, the eccentric prophet of a new style, identified with this statue, talking to it, swearing at it, yelling at it: "Speak!"

▶ *Now pass into Room 15, with a large cutaway model of the dome suspended from the ceiling.*

Gallery of the Dome (Galleria della Cupola)

Room 15 is dedicated to the dome that defined the Florentine Renaissance (and the man who built it). Designed by Filippo Brunelleschi (1377-1446), the dome was the final component of the cathedral complex' construction. Start by watching a fine short video about Brunelleschi's masterpiece (runs constantly, alternating between English and Italian).

Donatello's eccentric prophet *Habakkuk*

Jeremiah smolders as Jerusalem burns.

► *Now find the following items.*

Tools and Scaffolding

The dome weighs an estimated 80 million pounds—as much as the entire population of Florence—so Brunelleschi had to design special tools and machines to lift and work all that stone. (The lantern alone—which caps the dome—is a marble building nearly as tall as the Baptistery.) You'll see sun-dried bricks, brick molds, rope, a tool belt, compasses, stone pincers, and various pulleys for lifting.

Although no scaffolding supported the dome itself, the stonemasons needed exterior scaffolding to stand on as they worked. Support timbers were stuck into postholes in the drum (some are visible on the church today).

The dome rose in rings. First, the workers stacked a few blocks of white marble to create part of the ribs, then connected the ribs with horizontal crosspieces before filling in the space with red brick, in a herringbone pattern. When the ring was complete and self-supporting, they'd move the scaffolding up and do another section.

Models of the Cupola and Lantern
(Modello Architettonico della Lanterna della Cupola)

These wooden models, done by Brunelleschi, show the dome he was constructing, including the top portion that would cap it. Brunelleschi's actual dome, a feat of engineering that was both functional and beautiful, put mathematics in stone. It rises 330 feet from the ground, with eight white, pointed-arch ribs filled in with red brick and capped with a lantern, or cupola, to hold it all in place.

In designing the dome, Brunelleschi faced a number of challenges. The dome had to cover a gaping 140-foot hole in the roof of the church (a drag on rainy Sundays), a hole too wide to be spanned by the wooden scaffolding that traditionally supported a dome under construction. (An earlier architect suggested supporting the dome with a great mound of dirt inside the church...filled with coins, so peasants would later cart it away for free.) In addition, the eight-sided "drum" that the dome was to rest on was too weak to support its weight, and there were no side buildings on the church on which to attach Gothic-style buttresses.

The solution was a dome within a dome, leaving a hollow space between to make the structure lighter. And the dome had to be

Model of the lantern that caps the Duomo

Brunelleschi, multitalented Renaissance Man

self-supporting, both while being built and when finished, so as not to require buttresses.

Brunelleschi used wooden models such as these to demonstrate his ideas to skeptical approval committees.

▶ *Now consider the remarkable man who built the dome, by pondering his "portrait," made on his deathbed.*

Brunelleschi's Death Mask (Maschera Funebre)

Brunelleschi was uniquely qualified to create the dome. Trained in sculpture, he gave it up in disgust after losing the gig for the Baptistery doors. In Rome, he visualized placing the Pantheon on top of Florence's Duomo, and dissected the Pantheon's mathematics and engineering.

In 1420 Brunelleschi was declared *capomaestro* of the dome project. He was a jack-of-all-trades and now master of all as well, overseeing every aspect of the dome, the lantern, and the machinery to build it all.

The dome was completed in 16 short years, capping 150 years of construction on the church. Brunelleschi enjoyed the dedication ceremonies, but he died before the lantern was completed. His legacy is a dome that stands as a proud symbol of man's ingenuity, proving that art and science can unite to make beauty.

▶ *With the dome nearing completion, the Florentines began to decorate the church interior. Let's see some exquisite pieces. Exit Room 15 into Room 22 and turn left into Room 23 to see the...*

Room of the Cantorie (Sala delle Cantorie)

This room displays two marble choir lofts (*cantorie*) that once sat above the sacristy doors inside the Duomo. Both are from the 1430s. The one on the right is by Luca della Robbia, the one on the left by Donatello.

Luca della Robbia, *Cantoria*, 1430-c. 1438

After almost 150 years of construction, the cathedral was nearly done, and the Opera del Duomo, the workshop in charge, began preparing the interior for the celebration. Brunelleschi hired a little-known sculptor, 30-year-old Luca della Robbia, to make this *cantoria,* a balcony choir box for singers in the cathedral. It sums up the exuberance of the Quattrocento. The panels are a celebration of music, song, and dance performed by toddlers, children, and teenagers.

The *cantoria* brings Psalm 150 ("Praise ye the Lord") to life like a YouTube video. Starting in the upper left, the banner reads *"Laudate..."*—"Praise the Lord"—while children laugh and dance to the sound of trumpets *("sono Tubae")* and guitars, autoharps, and tambourines *("Psaltero... Cythera... Timpano")*. In the next level down, kids dance ring-around-the-rosy, a scene in the round on an almost-flat surface, showing front, back, and in-between poses. At bottom right, the Psalm ends: "Everybody praise the Lord!" Della Robbia's choir box was a triumph, a celebration of Florence's youthful boom time. (The Della Robbia family is best known for their colorful glazed terra-cotta, some of which you'll likely see here in the Duomo Museum and around town.)

Donatello, *Cantoria*, 1433-c. 1440

If Della Robbia's balcony looks like afternoon recess, Donatello's looks like an all-night rave. Donatello's figures are sketchier, murky and frenetic, as the dancing kids hurl themselves around the balcony. Imagine candles lighting this as the scenes seem to come to life.

Recently returned from a trip to Rome, Donatello carved in the style of classical friezes of dancing *putti* (chubby, playful toddlers). This choir box stood in a dark area of the Duomo, so Donatello chose

Choir boxes from the original church: Della Robbia's (left) is exuberant, Donatello's is dark.

Pop. 100,000...But Still a Small Town

At the dawn of the Renaissance, Florence was bursting with creative geniuses, all of whom knew each other and worked together. For example, after Ghiberti won the bronze-door competition, Brunelleschi took teenage Donatello with him to Rome. Donatello returned to join Ghiberti's workshop. Ghiberti helped Brunelleschi with dome plans. Brunelleschi, Donatello, and Luca della Robbia collaborated on the Pazzi Chapel. And so on, and so on.

colorful mosaics and marbles to catch the eye, while purposely leaving the dancers unfinished and shadowy, tangled figures flitting inside. In the dim light, worshippers swore they saw them move.

▶ *Now let's bring the Duomo up to the church we see today. Backtrack through Room 22, and down the corridor of Room 26. You'll pass by various diagrams, paintings, and photos that chart the multicentury...*

Evolution of the Facade

In 1587, the Duomo's medieval facade by Arnolfo di Cambio was considered hopelessly outdated and torn down like so much old linoleum. But work on a replacement never got off the ground, and the front of the church sat bare for nearly 300 years while church fathers debated proposal after proposal by many famous architects—that is, the designs in this room.

Finally, in the 1800s, as Italy was unifying and filled with a can-do spirit, there was a push to finish the facade. Emilio De Fabris (portrait near the end of Room 26) built a neo-Gothic facade (dedicated in 1887) that echoed the original work of Arnolfo. Critics charged that De Fabris' facade was too retro and ornate, but it was the style beloved by Ghiberti, Donatello, Brunelleschi, and the industrious citizens of Florence's Quattrocento, who saw it as Florence's finest art gallery.

Rest of the Museum

Browse the two floors above this one—they're accessed by a staircase near Room 15 (the Brunelleschi room). The second floor has a number of wooden models of various proposals for the facade—all rejected.

Don't miss the Terrazza Brunelleschiana on the third floor—an

Artisans restore old sculptures and craft new pieces at the Opera del Duomo art studio.

outdoor terrace with an up-close, rooftop view of the Duomo. It's an ideal place to pause at the end of your visit (and use the adjacent WC) and reflect on the engineering marvel that inspired so many other architects and marked the pinnacle of Renaissance achievement.

Art Studio

After leaving the Duomo Museum, make one more stop for a fascinating behind-the-scenes peek at the Duomo's restoration workshop: Head to the left around the back of the Duomo to find Via dello Studio #23a (see map on page 104). You can look through the open doorway and see workers sculpting new statues, restoring old ones, or making exact copies. It's run by the Opera del Duomo, the organization that does the continual work required to keep the cathedral's art in good repair (*opera* is Italian for "work"). They're carrying on an artistic tradition that dates back to the days of Brunelleschi. The "opera" continues.

Sights

Florence has more high-powered sights and museums per kilometer than any city in Europe. Though the city is small, I've clustered sights into "neighborhoods" (e.g., North of the Duomo) to make your sightseeing more efficient. Remember that some of Florence's biggest sights (marked with a ✪) are described in much more detail in the individual walks and tours chapters.

A few quick tips: Make reservations or buy a Firenze Card to avoid lines at the Uffizi and Accademia. Many sights are closed Monday and close early on Sunday. Some sights have erratic hours, so get the most up-to-date list at the Florence TI or online. Modest dress is required at some churches. See page 164 for more tips.

Despite the crowds, Florence prides itself on its gentility and grace under pressure. Be flexible.

Florence

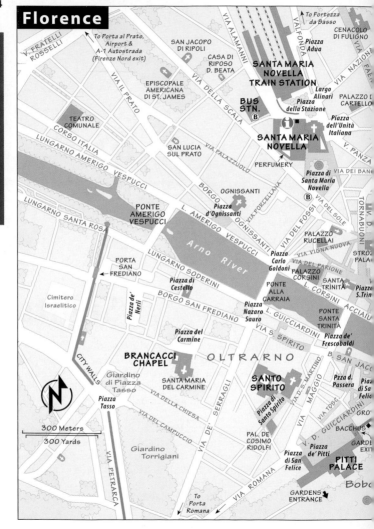

To Fortezza
da Basso

CENACOLO
DI FULIGNO

*Piazza
Adua*

VIA ALAMANNI

VALFONDA

VIA NAZIONALE

VIA FAE

V. FRATELLI
ROSSELLI

To Porta al Prato,
Airport &
A-1 Autostrada
(Firenze Nord exit)

SAN JACOPO
DI RIPOLI

CASA DI
RIPOSO
D. BEATA

VIA DELLA SCALA

EPISCOPALE
AMERICANA
DI ST. JAMES

VIA IL PRATO

SANTA MARIA
NOVELLA
TRAIN STATION

*Largo
Alinari*

PALAZZO D
CARTELLO

*Piazza
della Stazione*

BUS
STN.
B

*Piazza
dell'Unità
Italiana*

V. PANZA

TEATRO
COMUNALE

CORSO ITALIA

LUNGARNO AMERIGO VESPUCCI

SAN LUCIA
SUL PRATO

VIA PALAZZUOLO

SANTA MARIA
NOVELLA

PERFUMERY

*Piazza di
Santa Maria
Novella*

VIA DEI BAN

B

VIA DEL SOLE

BORGO OGNISSANTI

OGNISSANTI

*Piazza
d'Ognissanti*

L. AMERIGO VESPUCCI

VIA FORCELLANA

PALAZZO
RUCELLAI

VIA VIGNA NUOVA

TORNABUONI

LV. D
STRO
PALA

LUNGARNO SANTA ROSA

PONTE
AMERIGO
VESPUCCI

Arno River

*Piazza
Carlo
Goldoni*

VIA DEL PARIONE

PALAZZO
CORSINI

SANTA
TRINITÀ

*Piazza
S.Trin*

PORTA
SAN
FREDIANO

LUNGARNO SODERINI

*Piazza di
Cestello*

BORGO SAN FREDIANO

PONTE
ALLA
CARRAIA

L. CORSINI

ACCIAIU

Cimitero
Israelitico

*Piazza de'
Neri*

*Piazza
Nazaro
Sauro*

L. GUICCIARDINI

PONTE
SANTA
TRINITÀ

*Piazza de'
Frescobaldi*

VIA S. SPIRITO

B. SAN JAC

CITY WALLS

*Piazza del
Carmine*

OLTRARNO

B. SAN JAC

BRANCACCI
CHAPEL

*Giardino
di Piazza
Tasso*

SANTA MARIA
DEL CARMINE

VIA DE SERRAGLI

VIA DELLA CHIESA

SANTO
SPIRITO

VIA D. S. MARTINO

*Pza d.
Passera*

*Piaz
di Sa
Felic*

N

*Piazza
Tasso*

VIA DEL CAMPUCCIO

*Piazza di
Santa Spirito*

VIA S. MAGGIO

VIA TOSC

D. GUICCIARDINI

*Piazza
de' Pitti*

BACCHUS◆

GARDE
EXIT

300 Meters

300 Yards

Giardino
Torrigiani

VIA PETRARCA

PAL. DE
COSIMO
RIDOLFI

VIA ROMANA

*Piazza
di San
Felice*

PITTI
PALACE

Bob

To
Porta
Romana

GARDENS
ENTRANCE

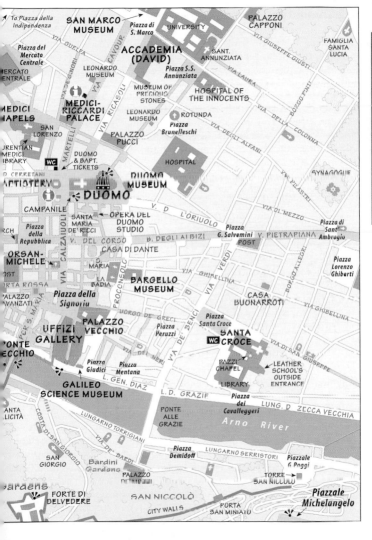

The Duomo and Nearby Sights

Largely pedestrian-only and geared for tourists, this is Florence's sightseeing core. To walk from the Duomo to the Arno takes 10 minutes, max. Many sights lie along the north-south spine of Via Calzaiouli, easily connected by my ✪ Renaissance Walk and 🎧 free audio tour.

▲▲ Duomo (Cattedrale di Santa Maria del Fiore)

Florence's huge Gothic cathedral, or Duomo (from Latin domus— "house" of God), was built in medieval times and later topped with Filippo Brunelleschi's magnificent red-and-white dome that helped define the Renaissance.

The interior is huge and historic, but not worth a long wait to get in. The 500-foot-long, gray-and-white nave is the third longest in Christendom. Find busts of the Duomo's architects. Arnolfo di Cambio (left wall) started the church in 1296. Giotto (right wall) designed the Campanile (1330s). Brunelleschi (right wall) capped the church with the famous dome (c. 1450). Finally, Emilio de Fabris (left wall) added the pink-green-white facade (1870s).

Above the main entrance is a huge clock, painted by Paolo Uccello (1443). It's a 24-hour clock, starting with sunset as the first hour, and turning counterclockwise.

Uccello's painting of John Hawkwood (left wall, colored green) wowed Florence with the 3-D illusion of an equestrian statue painted on a flat surface. A few steps up the nave is Florence's great poet Dante, with the city skyline in the distance.

At the altar, gaze up 300 feet into Brunelleschi's dome, which had to span a gaping 140-foot-wide hole. The vast dome is painted with the *Last Judgment* (by Vasari and Zuccari), where the dead rise into a multilevel heaven to be judged by a radiant Christ.

▶ *Free. A combo-ticket (€15) covering the other Duomo sights can be purchased inside the cathedral or at the ticket office opposite the Baptistery (Firenze Card holders must go to the ticket office to obtain a free combo-ticket to visit Duomo sights). Open Mon-Fri 10:00-17:00 (Thu until 16:30), Sat 10:00-16:45, Sun 13:30-16:45. Modest dress code enforced. Tel. 055-230-2885, www.museumflorence.com.*

Lines: Because the church is free (and therefore not "covered" by the Firenze Card), lines can be long, but they move fast.

✪ For more on the Duomo, see the Renaissance Walk.

▲ Climbing the Duomo's Dome

Climb 463 steps to see a grand view into the cathedral from the base of the dome; Brunelleschi's innovative "dome-within-a-dome" construction; and finally, a glorious Florence-wide view from the top.

▸ €15 combo-ticket covers all Duomo sights; also covered by Firenze Card; with either, must reserve dome-climb time when obtaining your ticket (or better, book well ahead at www.museumflorence.com). Open Mon-Fri 8:30-20:00, Sat 8:30-17:40, Sun 13:00-16:00. Enter from outside the church on the north side. Tel. 055-230-2885.

✪ For more on the dome, see the Renaissance Walk.

▲ Campanile (Giotto's Tower)

The 270-foot bell tower was designed by the great painter Giotto and decorated with statues by Donatello and others. Climb its 414 steps (faster and less claustrophobic than climbing the Duomo's dome) for equally good views, including a view of that magnificent dome to boot.

▸ €15 combo-ticket covers all Duomo sights; also covered by Firenze Card. Open daily 8:30-20:00; last entry 40 minutes before closing.

✪ For more on the Campanile, see the Renaissance Walk.

▲ Baptistery

Nearly 1,000 years old, this building is most famous for its bronze doors. Lorenzo Ghiberti helped launch Renaissance perspective by depicting 3-D scenes on the doors' almost-flat surface. His north doors won a famous competition, while his east doors (facing the Duomo) were hailed by Michelangelo as the "Gates of Paradise."

Inside, sit and savor the medieval mosaic ceiling, where it's always Judgment Day and Jesus is giving the ultimate thumbs-up and thumbs-down.

▸ €15 combo-ticket covers all Duomo sights; also covered by Firenze Card. The interior is open Mon-Sat 8:15-20:00, Sun 8:30-14:00. The bronze doors are on the exterior, so they are always viewable. Tel. 055-230-2885.

✪ For more on the Baptistery, see the Renaissance Walk.

✪ For more on Ghiberti's famous doors, see the Duomo Museum Tour (with the original "Gates of Paradise").

▲▲▲ Duomo Museum (Museo dell'Opera del Duomo)

Located behind the church (at Via del Proconsolo 9), the recently spiffed-up cathedral museum is filled with a late Michelangelo *Pietà*, expressive Donatello statues, and Ghiberti's original bronze "Gates of Paradise" panels.

✪ See the Duomo Museum Tour.

▲▲▲ Bargello (Museo Nazionale del Bargello)

This underappreciated sculpture museum has Donatello's prepubescent *David,* Michelangelo's *Bacchus,* and rooms of Medici treasures.

✪ See the Bargello Tour and 🎧 download my free audio tour.

Casa di Dante (Dante's House)

Dante Alighieri (1265-1321), the poet who gave us *The Divine Comedy,* is the Shakespeare of Italy, the father of the modern Italian language, and the face on the country's €2 coin.

Dante lovers (but not everyone else) will appreciate this small, low-tech museum. It follows his life from his christening in Florence's Baptistery, to his spiritual awakening upon meeting his muse Beatrice, and the bitter years of political exile—never again to return to Florence. Homeless in Italy, Dante wrote his magnum opus, *The Divine Comedy,* which traces a pilgrim's journey through Hell and Purgatory, until—guided by a heavenly Beatrice—he's received into Paradise. For his landmark work, some call Dante the father of the Renaissance.

▸ *€4, covered by Firenze Card. April-Sept daily 10:00-18:00; Oct-March Tue-Sun 10:00-17:00, closed Mon. Near the Bargello at Via Santa Margherita 1. Tel. 055-219-416, www.museocasadidante.it.*

▲ Orsanmichele Church

The exterior is a virtual sculpture gallery of Renaissance art (especially Donatello's *St. George*), and the peaceful interior has a glorious Gothic tabernacle.

✪ See the Renaissance Walk.

▲ Mercato Nuovo (a.k.a. the Straw Market)

This open-air loggia (c. 1550), originally a silk and straw market, is now a rustic yet touristy market. Its souvenirs are similar to the San Lorenzo market, but with firmer prices. Notice the circled X in the center, marking the spot where people landed after being dropped from the ceiling as punishment for bankruptcy. Find *Il Porcellino* (a statue of a wild boar), rub his nose, and "feed" him a coin to ensure your return to Florence. Finish your visit at the food wagon in back, enjoying a traditional tripe sandwich—a local favorite.

▶ *Open daily 9:00-18:30. Located three blocks north of Ponte Vecchio on Via Calimala.*

▲ Piazza della Repubblica

Lined with venerable cafés and high-fashion stores, this square has been a center of Florence for millennia. In Roman times, it was a fort at the intersection of the two main roads (marked today by the square's lone column). In 1571, Cosimo I de' Medici had the area walled in and made into the Jewish ghetto. If you venture outside the piazza, you get a sense of what the old neighborhood was like—a tangle of narrow, winding lanes dotted with medieval towers. In the late 19th century, the area was razed to create this spacious square, with a huge triumphal arch celebrating the unification of Italy.

Today, people sip drinks at outdoor cafes, shop at the local La Rinascente department store, or enjoy a reasonably priced coffee on the store's rooftop terrace, with great Duomo and city views.

▲ Palazzo Davanzati

This five-story, late-medieval tower house offers a rare look at a

Piazza della Repubblica, long a main intersection, is now a square surrounded by elegant cafés.

typical noble dwelling from the 14th century. The exterior is festooned with horse-tethering rings, torch holders, and poles for hanging laundry or flying flags. Inside, though the furnishings are pretty sparse, you'll see richly painted walls, fireplaces, a lace display, and even an indoor "outhouse."

▶ *€6, covered by Firenze Card. Open Tue-Sat 8:15-13:50, plus the first, third, and fifth Sun and second and fourth Mon of each month. Located at Via Porta Rossa 13. Tel. 055-238-8610, www.bargellomusei. beniculturali.it.*

▲▲▲ Uffizi Gallery

The greatest collection of Italian paintings anywhere features masterpieces by Giotto, Leonardo, Raphael, Titian, and Michelangelo, plus a roomful of Botticellis, including the *Birth of Venus*. Watch Western art evolve from stiff medieval altarpieces to three-dimensional Renaissance realism.

✪ See the Uffizi Gallery Tour and ∩ download my free audio tour.

▲▲ Palazzo Vecchio

This castle-like fortress with the 300-foot spire dominates Florence's main square. In Renaissance times, it was the Town Hall, where citizens pioneered the once-radical notion of self-rule. Its official name—Palazzo della Signoria—refers to the elected members of the city council. In 1540, the tyrant Cosimo I de' Medici made the building his personal palace, redecorating the interior in lavish style. Today the building functions once again as the Town Hall.

Entry to the ground-floor courtyard is free—step inside and feel the essence of the Medici.

Paying customers can see Cosimo's (fairly) lavish royal apartments, decorated with (fairly) top-notch paintings and statues by Michelangelo and Donatello. The highlight is the Grand Hall, a 13,000-square-foot hall lined with huge frescoes of battle scenes by Giorgio Vasari. You can climb the tower for great views.

▶ *Museum-€10, tower climb-€10, museum plus tower-€14, excavations-€4, combo-ticket for all three-€18, covered by Firenze Card. Open Fri-Wed 9:00-23:00 (Oct-March until 19:00, Thu 9:00-14:00, ticket office closes one hour earlier. Tel. 055-276-8224, www.musefirenze.it.*

✪ See the Renaissance Walk.

Palazzo Vecchio, full of art and history

Galileo Science Museum has his finger.

▲ Ponte Vecchio

Florence's most famous bridge has long been lined with shops—origi nally butcher shops, and now selling gold and silver.

☼ For more about the bridge, see the Renaissance Walk.

▲▲ Galileo Science Museum
(Museo Galilei e Istituto di Storia della Scienza)

Enough art, already! For a change of pace from statues and Madonnas, visit this collection of scientific curios, clocks, telescopes, maps, and turn-the-crank electrical contraptions, from A.D. 1000 to 1900. The museum is friendly, never crowded, and—ahhh!—wonderfully air-conditioned.

You'll see instruments of that trendsetting family, the Medici, who always seemed at the forefront of Europe's arts and sciences (Room I). Room II shows quadrants and astrolabes—navigation tools you'd point toward the horizon to triangulate your position relative to the stars. Room III has an 11-foot-tall armillary sphere, showing the earth surrounded by orbiting planets—the earth-centered view of the cosmos of medieval times.

The museum's highlight is the exhibit on Galileo Galilei (1564-1642), the groundbreaking scientist from Tuscany. Galileo was the first earthling to see the moons of Jupiter, using a homemade, 30-power telescope (the museum has several of his telescopes). You'll see his experiments on pendulum motion, falling objects, and an early thermoscope. Galileo was famously punished by the Church for claiming that the earth revolved around the sun. Appropriately, the museum's most talked-about exhibit is a jar containing Galileo's middle finger, raised eternally upward for all those blind to science.

▶ *€9, €22 family ticket, covered by Firenze Card. Open Wed-Mon 9:30-18:00, Tue 9:30-13:00. Located a block east of the Uffizi, at Piazza dei Giudici 1. Tel. 055-265-311, www.museogalileo.it.*

North of the Duomo

There are two sightseeing clusters—sights near the Accademia, and sights around the Basilica of San Lorenzo. Both are an easy 10-minute walk from the Duomo.

▲▲▲ Accademia (Galleria dell'Accademia)

The star is Michelangelo's *David,* the consummate Renaissance statue of the buff, biblical shepherd boy taking on the giant. You'll also see the master's powerful (unfinished) *Prisoners.*

✪ See the Accademia Tour and ⌂ download my free audio tour.

▲▲ Museum of San Marco (Museo di San Marco)

This 15th-century monastery houses the greatest collection anywhere of the early Renaissance painter Fra Angelico (c. 1400-1455). Fra Angelico (the "Angelic Brother") was the monastery's prior, known for his sweetness and humility (and beatified in 1984).

On the ground floor, the Hospice displays a dozen major altarpieces. His work fuses medieval styles (religious subjects, elaborate frames, serene faces, gold halos, and pious atmospheres) with Renaissance realism. Heavenly scenes are set in the Tuscan landscape, amid real-life flowers, trees, and distant hillsides. He uses bright primary colors (red-blue-yellow-gold) and meticulous, etched-in-glass detail. It's all evenly lit (with no moody shadows), creating a beautiful, mystical world—paintings that glow from within like stained-glass windows.

Upstairs on the first floor are the monks' cells, or living quarters. Many were frescoed by Fra Angelico, particularly the 10 cells on your left as you venture down the corridor.

Don't miss the cells of Girolamo Savonarola (1452-1498), a later prior. This charismatic monk rode in from the Christian right, threw out the Medici, turned Florence into a theocracy, and sponsored "bonfires of the vanities" to burn books, paintings, and so on. You'll see his austere possessions—his simple wool clothes, blue Dominican cloak, rosary, crucifix, Bible, desk, and hair-shirt girdle. Finally, there's a stick snatched from the bonfire that burned Savonarola himself when Florence decided to change channels.

Fra Angelico work at Museum of San Marco   San Lorenzo church, home to Medici Chapels

▶ €4, covered by Firenze Card. Open Tue-Fri 8:15-13:50, Sat 8:15-16:50; also open 8:15-13:50 on first, third, and fifth Mon and 8:15-16:50 on second and fourth Sun of each month. Reservations possible but unnecessary. No bag check, and large bags not allowed. Located on Piazza San Marco, a block north of the Accademia. Tel. 055-238-8608. 🎧 Download my free audio tour.

Museum of Precious Stones
(Museo dell'Opificio delle Pietre Dure)

This unusual gem of a museum features exquisite mosaics of inlaid marble and other stones. The Medici loved colorful stone tabletops and floors, some featuring landscapes and portraits (find Cosimo I in Room I). Upstairs, you'll see wooden workbenches from the Medici workshop (1588), complete with foot-powered saws and drills. Rockhounds can browse 500 different stones (lapis lazuli, quartz, agate, marble, and so on) and the tools used to cut and inlay them.

▶ €4, covered by Firenze Card. Open Mon-Sat 8:15-14:00, closed Sun. English descriptions. Located around the corner from the Accademia at Via degli Alfani 78, tel. 055-265-1357, www.opificiodellepietredure.it.

Basilica of San Lorenzo

This red-brick dome—which looks like the Duomo's little sister—was the Medici family's home church. The church anchors a complex of sights, described next: The Laurentian Medici Library (off a pleasant cloister) is along the left side and the Medici Chapels entrance is around back.

The church facade is rough and exposed brick, unfinished because Pope Leo X (also a Medici) pulled the plug on Michelangelo's proposed makeover. Inside, the fresh spirit of 1420s Florence shines in Brunelleschi's perfectly symmetrical gray-and-white arches and diffused light. The Medici coat of arms (with the round pills of these "medics") decorates the ceiling, and everywhere are images of St. Lawrence, the Medici patron saint who was martyred on a grill.

Highlights of the church include two finely sculpted Donatello pulpits (in the nave) and Filippo Lippi's *Annunciation* (left transept). The Old Sacristy (far left corner)—designed by Brunelleschi, and decorated by Donatello and Luca della Robbia—was a Medici burial chapel. Over the Sacristy's altar, a painted dome shows the exact arrangement of the heavens on July 4, 1442. Why that date? Scholars continue to speculate.

The Laurentian Medici Library, designed by Michelangelo, is best known for the impressive staircase, which widens imperceptibly as it descends. Michelangelo also did the surrounding walls, featuring empty niches, scrolls, and oddly tapering pilasters. Climb the stairs and enter the Reading Room—a long, rectangular hall with a coffered-wood ceiling—designed by Michelangelo to host scholars enjoying the Medici's collection of manuscripts.

▶ *€6, €8.50 combo-ticket covers Laurentian Library, covered by Firenze Card. Buy tickets just inside cloister to the left of the facade. Church and crypt open Mon-Sat 10:00-17:30, Sun 13:30-17:30, closed Sun Nov-Feb; library open Mon, Wed, and Fri 8:00-14:00, Tue and Thu 8:00-17:30, closed Sat-Sun.*

▲▲ Medici Chapels (Cappelle Medicee)

The burial site of the Medici family stars Michelangelo's New Sacristy (1520-1534). Michelangelo had spent his teen years living with the Medici, and here he paid them final tribute with monumental architecture, tombs, and brooding statues.

Your visit leads first into the big, domed (non-Michelangelo) Chapel of Princes (1602-1743), honoring later generations of Medici rulers.

Michelangelo's New Sacristy houses three Medici tombs. The Tomb of Lorenzo II (left wall, as you enter) depicts the grandson of Lorenzo the Magnificent as a Roman general atop a curved sarcophagus. Its two reclining statues are *Dusk* (a man, reflecting on the day's events) and *Dawn* (a woman, stirring restlessly after a long night). The Tomb of Giuliano (right wall) honors the son of Lorenzo the Magnificent. It features *Day* (a man, with each limb twisting in a different direction) and *Night* (a well-polished woman with coconut-shell breasts who does a crossover sit-up in her sleep). Together, the four statues represent the passage of Time.

The humble tomb on the entrance wall honors Lorenzo the Magnificent and his brother. Originally meant to be the grandest tomb, it was left unfinished, now topped with a Madonna and Child by Michelangelo. The Sacristy's altar wall has black doodles (behind glass), presumably by Michelangelo. Michelangelo eventually abandoned the New Sacristy project, leaving it to be pieced together by assistants.

Michelangelo intended the room to symbolize how Time (the four reclining statues) kills mortal men (Lorenzo II and

SIGHTS

New Sacristy

```
                    ↙ SKETCHES ↘
                      ┌─────┐
                      │ALTAR│
                      └─────┘
 L                                    G
 O                                    I
 R    ▌DAWN            NIGHT▌         U
 E                                    L
 N                                    I
 Z    ▌DUSK            DAY ▌          A
 O                                    N
 II                                   O

              MEDICI
              MADONNA
           ┌──────────────┐
           │ LORENZO THE  │
           │ MAGNIFICENT &│
           │HIS BROTHER GIULIANO│
           └──────────────┘
       From
   Chapel of Princes
     & Entrance           (N)

   [Not to Scale]
```

Giuliano), but through God's Grace (Madonna and Child), we can rise from the Earth (the ground floor) into the light (the windows and lantern) of Heaven (the geometrically perfect dome). Until then, Michelangelo's earth-bound statues squirm restlessly, pondering mortality but unable to come to terms with it.

▶ €8, covered by Firenze Card. Open Tue-Sat 8:15-17:00, Nov-March until 13:50; also open second and fourth Mon and first, third, and fifth Sun of each month; last entry 40 minutes before closing. Reservations are possible but unnecessary. Modest dress required. Enter at back side of Basilica of San Lorenzo. Tel. 055-238-8602, www.bargellomusei. beniculturali.it.

▲ San Lorenzo Market

The vast open-air market sprawls in the streets just north of the Basilica of San Lorenzo. Find T-shirts, scarves, cheap souvenirs, and

Day and *Night* recline in the Medici Chapels.

Medici-Riccardi Palace, the Medici home

leather goods of varying quality. Many of the leather stalls are run by Iranians selling South American leather that was tailored in Italy; a few more-reputable leather shops with permanent addresses are nearby. Prices are soft, so go ahead and bargain.

▶ *Open daily 9:00-19:00, closed Mon in winter.*

▲ Mercato Centrale (Central Market)

Florence's giant iron-and-glass-covered central market, a wonderland of picturesque produce, exudes a Florentine elegance. Enjoy generous free samples, watch pasta being made, graze fun eateries, and explore the sleek upscale food court upstairs. It's perfect for assembling a picnic, people-watching, and acquiring culinary souvenirs. Explore. You'll see parts of the cow you'd never dream of eating (no, that's not a turkey neck).

▶ *Open Mon-Fri 7:00-14:00, Sat until 17:00, closed Sun.*

▲ Medici-Riccardi Palace (Palazzo Medici-Riccardi)

Built in 1444, this palace was home to the illustrious Medici family, including Lorenzo the Magnificent and Cosimo the Elder, as well as Michelangelo (who spent his teenage years here studying art). The palace also played host to many visitors, including Leonardo da Vinci (who played the lute at Medici parties) and Botticelli (who studied the palace art). Soak up fading remnants of this historical ambience in the courtyard and sculpture-studded garden.

Upstairs is the highlight—the Chapel of the Magi. Benozzo Gozzoli's colorful frescoes of *The Journey of the Magi* (1459) are a snapshot of Renaissance Florence. The three Magi are dressed in the latest 15th-century fashions, and parade on horseback through a

Best Viewpoints

- The Campanile and the Duomo's dome (next to each other) and the tower at the Palazzo Vecchio offer the best views within the city.
- Piazzale Michelangelo (and San Miniato Church, above it) overlooks the city and the Duomo from across the Arno River.
- Fiesole, a small town north of Florence, has panoramic hilltop views.
- La Rinascente department store, on Piazza Repubblica, has a reasonably priced top-floor terrace café.
- The Uffizi's café has cappuccino-friendly views of Palazzo Vecchio and the Duomo.

SIGHTS

green, spacious Tuscan landscape. Find famous Medici in the frescoes. On the biggest wall is Cosimo the Elder (in a red hat, riding behind the curly-haired king). Behind Cosimo, find 10-year-old Lorenzo the Magnificent (sixth in from the left, with red cap, scoop nose, bowl-cut hair, and intense gaze). Above Lorenzo (and slightly to the left) is Gozzoli himself.

The palace also has a few partially furnished rooms, a Madonna and Child by Fra Filippo Lippi, and a Baroque ceiling fresco by Luca Giordano.

▶ €10, cash only, covered by Firenze Card. Open Thu-Tue 8:30-19:00, closed Wed. The ticket entrance is north of the main gated entrance. Videoguide €4. Located at Via Cavour 3, a long block north of the Duomo. Tel. 055-276-0340, www.palazzo-medici.it.

Leonardo Museums

Two different-but-similar entrepreneurial establishments several blocks apart (Le Macchine di Leonardo da Vinci and Museo Leonardo da Vinci) show off reproductions of Leonardo's ingenious inventions and experiments. While there are no actual historic artifacts, you can see a full-size armored tank, walk into a chamber of mirrors, operate a rotating crane, or watch experiments in flying. There are English descriptions, and you're encouraged to play with the models—great for kids. Either museum is fun for anyone who wants to crank the shaft of Leonardo's fertile imagination.

▶ Admission to each museum is €7 for adults, €5 for kids 6 and old-

free for kids 5 and under, €1-2 discount with this book. **Le Macchine di Leonardo da Vinci** *open daily 9:30-19:30; Nov-March 10:30-18:30. Located in Galleria Michelangelo at Via Cavour 21. Tel. 055-295-264, www.museoleonardodavincifirenze.com.* **Museo Leonardo da Vinci** *open daily 10:00-19:00, Nov-March until 18:00. Located at Via dei Servi 66 red. Tel. 055-282-966, www.mostredileonardo.com.*

East of the Duomo

The landmark of this less-visited area is Santa Croce Church, a gathering spot in this (slightly rundown) neighborhood.

▲▲ Santa Croce Church

One of Florence's biggest and oldest churches (begun 1294), Santa Croce houses groundbreaking art and the tombs of great Florentines. The spacious 375-foot nave is lined with tall columns and wide, airy arches. On the left side is the tomb of Galileo, the scientist who served Florence's Grand Duke. On the right side are Michelangelo (who grew up a block west of here and attended Santa Croce), Dante (a memorial to the hometown poet), Machiavelli (who penned a how-to manual on hardball politics), and Rossini (who composed the *William Tell Overture*).

To the right of the main altar is Giotto's *Death of St. Francis* (c. 1325). With simple but eloquent gestures, Francis' brothers kneel to bid the charismatic monk a sad farewell. It's one of the first expressions of human emotion in modern painting, foreshadowing the Renaissance. You'll find an impressive wooden ceiling decorated with Franciscan saints in the sacristy (first door on the left from the main church) and Cimabue's expressive (if flood-damaged) Crucifixion (before 1288). A hallway leads to a leather school, where poor people make leather goods for sale.

Exit into the cloister, with the domed Pazzi Chapel (1430). Brunelleschi's circle-in-square design, simple white-and-gray color scheme, and perfect geometry capture the Renaissance in miniature. The Museum (included with admission) has Gaddi's 1,300-square-foot *Tree of the Cross* and *Last Supper*. Medieval monks could sit be-
~~ath~~ this *Last Supper* and imagine they were eating in the company
s.

overed by Firenze Card. Open Mon-Sat 9:30-17:30, Sun 14:00-. Modest dress required. Located a 10-minute walk east of the

Santa Croce—tombs, frescoes, architecture

S. M. Novella—Masaccio's 3-D fresco

Palazzo Vecchio along Borgo de' Greci. Tel. 055-246-6105, www. santacroceopera.it.

Avoid lines by buying your ticket from the leather school at the back end of the church. To get there, head east along the left side of the church, enter the passageway at Via San Giuseppe 5 red, and follow signs through the small garden and parking lot to the low-key back entrance. Don't be shy—they want you to visit their store. Once inside, pass through the workshops to the sales room with the cash register, buy a church ticket, and head down the hallway that leads into the church.

▲ Casa Buonarroti (Michelangelo's House)

This museum standing on property once owned by Michelangelo displays some of Michelangelo's early, less-than-monumental statues and a few sketches.

Climb the stairs, where you come face-to-face with portraits (by his contemporaries) of 60-year old Michelangelo. Also displayed are Buonarroti family walking sticks and some leather slippers thought to be Michelangelo's.

The museum's highlight is two relief panels, Michelangelo's earliest known sculptures. Teenage Michelangelo carved the *Battle of the Centaurs* (1490-1492), a squirming tangle of battling nudes, showing his fascination with anatomy. He kept this in his personal collection all his life. *The Madonna of the Stairs* (c. 1490) is as contemplative as *Centaurs* is dramatic. Throughout his long career, bipolar Michelangelo veered between these two styles—moving or still, emotional or thoughtful, pagan or Christian.

In an adjoining room are the big wooden model (maybe by Michelangelo) of the never-completed facade of the Basilica of San

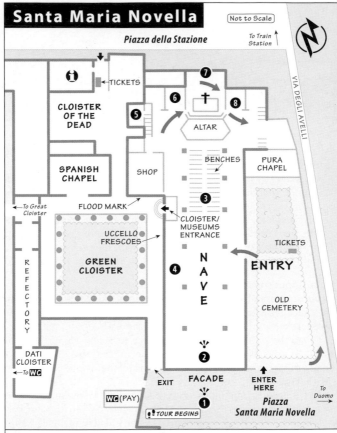

Santa Maria Novella

Not to Scale

Piazza della Stazione

To Train Station

VIA DEGLI AVELLI

TICKETS

CLOISTER OF THE DEAD

SPANISH CHAPEL

SHOP

FLOOD MARK

←To Great Cloister

REFECTORY

GREEN CLOISTER

UCCELLO FRESCOES

DATI CLOISTER

←To WC

WC (PAY)

ALTAR

BENCHES

PURA CHAPEL

CLOISTER/ MUSEUMS ENTRANCE

TICKETS

ENTRY

N A V E

OLD CEMETERY

EXIT FACADE ENTER HERE

To Duomo

Piazza Santa Maria Novella

TOUR BEGINS

1 View of Facade

2 View down the Nave

3 GIOTTO – Crucifixion

4 MASACCIO – The Trinity

5 ORCAGNA BROTHERS – Hell, Purgatory & Heaven

6 BRUNELLESCHI – Crucifixion

7 GHIRLANDAIO – Fresco Cycles of Mary and John the Baptist

8 FILIPPINO LIPPI – St. Philip at the Temple of Mars & St. John the Evangelist Raising Drusiana

SIGHTS

Lorenzo and a model of a never completed river god for the Medici Chapels. Back near the landing, a darkened room shows off some of Michelangelo's sketches (a rotating display of their vast collection). Vasari claimed that Michelangelo wanted to burn his preliminary sketches, lest anyone think him less than perfect. Another room near the landing displays small clay and wax models—some by Michelangelo, some by pupils—used to sketch out ideas for statues.

▶ *€6.50, covered by Firenze Card. Open Wed-Mon 10:00-17:00, closed Tue. Located at Via Ghibellina 70. Tel. 055-241-752, www.casabuonarroti.it.*

West of the Duomo

The train station and Church of Santa Maria Novella anchor this neighborhood a 10- to 15-minute walk from the Duomo.

▲▲ Church of Santa Maria Novella

This 13th-century Dominican church is chock-full of art from medieval to Mannerist, including Masaccio's 3-D breakthrough, *The Trinity.*

The green-and-white facade is by Alberti, c. 1460. Inside, look down the nave for an optical illusion—the columns converge and get shorter as they approach the altar, making the 330-foot nave look even longer.

In the nave hangs Giotto's *Crucifixion* (c. 1300), a study in understated tragedy. View Masaccio's *Trinity* (c. 1427, on the left wall) from about 20 feet away, standing on the shield with a crown. From this perspective, it appears that Masaccio has blown a nine-foot-high hole in the church wall, creating a chapel visited by God, Jesus on the cross, and several mourners. The chapel's checkerboard ceiling converges at the back to create the illusion of 3-D. Masaccio was the first painter since ancient times to portray real humans inhabiting a spacious, three-dimensional world.

In the left transept, a fresco of *Hell* (by the Orcagna brothers, c. 1350) shows naked souls begging for mercy a grim scene right out of the bubonic plague that killed half of Florence. Brunelleschi's realistic wooden crucifix hangs in a chapel to the left of the altar.

Behind the altar are frescoes by Ghirlandaio. Though ostensibly about John the Baptist, they're a virtual snapshot of everyday life in Florence, circa 1490. Florentines in their Sunday best parade through three-dimensional video-game landscapes of Renaissance architecture.

Finally, in Filippino Lippi's *St. Philip* (in the chapel to the right of the altar), the Christian saint battles the pagan god Mars by unleashing...a farting dragon. Believe it when you see it.

▶ *€5, covered by Firenze Card. Open Mon-Thu 9:00-19:00 (Oct-March until 17:30), Fri 11:00-19:00 (Oct-March until 17:30), Sat 9:00-17:30, Sun 13:00-17:30, last entry 45 minutes before closing. Audioguide-€5. Modest dress required. Tel. 055-219-257, www.SMN.it.*

Farmacia di Santa Maria Novella

Thick with the lingering aroma of centuries of spritzes, this palatial perfumery started as the herb garden of the Santa Maria Novella monks. Today it's a retail shop selling perfumes and herbal products. Well-known by locals for quality, it's extremely Florentine. Pick up the history sheet from the rack and wander deep into the shop. The third room dates from 1612 and offers a peek at one of Santa Maria Novella's cloisters. Gaze on its dreamy frescoes and imagine a time before Vespas and tourists.

▶ *Free, though shopping is encouraged. Open daily 9:00-20:00. Located a block west of Piazza Santa Maria Novella, 100 yards down Via della Scala at #16. Tel. 055-216-276, www.smnovella.com.*

South of the Arno River (Oltrarno)

The Arno River separates the city center from the Oltrarno—the neighborhood on the "other" (altro) side of the river. The two sides have historically been connected by the oldest bridge, Ponte Vecchio, lined with its characteristic shops.

Florence was born on the north bank (founded by the Romans in the first century B.C.). The Oltrarno grew in medieval times until, by Michelangelo's day, it was as extensive as the north side. It's always been Florence's poorer, working-class cousin. It's grittier, more local, with more artisan shops and fewer tourists. During midafternoon siesta, many streets look like a ghost town.

But it's an interesting look at a more authentic Florence, and it hosts several high-power sights—Pitti Palace, Santo Spirito Church, and Brancacci Chapel. To link these sights and see a few back lanes and local color, take the Oltrano Walk, described next.

▲ Oltrarno Walk

The map on page 124 traces the following route. The walk takes an hour (plus any sightseeing inside Pitti Palace, Brancacci C and Santo Spirito Church). It's best mornings or evenings—mi... noon is hot, and many churches and shops are closed.

Crossing the Ponte Vecchio, *turn right on Borgo San Jocopo*. Pause at the twin medieval towers, typical of the countless family towers that dotted 12th-century Florence's skyline. Hotel Lungarno's riverside viewpoint offers a great photo op of the Ponte Vecchio.

Turn left on tiny Via Toscanella, a quiet laundry-draped lane. You'll pass artisan shops plying generations-old trades—handmade furniture, leather goods, pottery, picture frames, bookbinding. If the door's open, step in and politely ask, *Posso guardare?*—"Can I take a look?"

At the end of Via Toscanella, to the left is Pitti Palace. *Turn right on Sdrucciolo de' Pitti* to reach Piazza Santo Spirito—with its church and trendy-but-seedy ambience.

From the far end of the piazza, *turn right on Via S. Agostino,* walking 5-10 minutes to the Brancacci Chapel. The neighborhoods around the church are considered the last surviving bits of old Florence.

With your back to the church, head straight, toward the river. *Turn right on Borgo San Frediano, which becomes Via di Santo Spirito.* A block in from the Arno River, this nearly traffic-free stretch of Via di Santo Spirito is home to shops run by a variety of artisans. When you reach Via Maggio, just before the delightful little 16th-century fountain and colorful produce shop, *head left onto Ponte Santa Trinità* for a great view of the cityscape flanking the Arno and the venerable Ponte Vecchio, where this walk began.

▲▲ Pitti Palace

The imposing Pitti Palace has many separate museums and two huge gardens. Trying to see it all can be more overwhelming than enjoyable. Focus on the Palatine Gallery—Florence's second-best collection of paintings—starring Raphael Madonnas and Titian portraits.

The plain and brutal façade is more than two football fields long. Enter and climb the stairs to reach the...

Palatine Gallery: To see the highlights, walk straight down the spine (avoiding side rooms), then make a U-turn and double back through a dozen more. In Room 1, a bust of Cosimo I de' Medici honors

Oltrarno Walk

#12 **B**

PONTE ALL
CARRAIA

Piazza
Nazaro
Sauro

LA CITÉ
LIBRERIA
CAFÉ

GELATERIA
LA CARRAIA

LUNGARN

To
Porta
San Frediano

BORGO SAN FREDIANO

Piazza degli
Scarlatti

VIA DELLEONE

V. DI SANTO SPIRIT

GEPP

BORGO STELLA

Piazza del
Carmine
7

VIA DELL'ORTO

SANTA
MONACA

VIA SANTA
MONACA

MAFFIA

VIA DE'

O L T R

BRANCACCI
CHAPEL

SANTA MARIA
DEL CARMINE

VIA D'ARDIGLIONE

VIA DE'

SERRAGLI

VIA S.AGOSTINO

200 Meters

200 Yards

VIA DELLA CHIESA

Piazza di
Santo Spirito

PAL.
DE COSIMO
RIDOLFI

TEG

1 Ponte Vecchio

2 Torre dei Barbadori, Torre
dei Belfredelli & Photo Op

3 Borgo San Jacopo

4 Via Toscanella

5 Pitti Palace

6 Piazza di Santo Spirito

7 Piazza del Carmine

8 Via di Santo Spirito
Artisan Shops

9 Ponte Santa Trinità

V. D. CALDAIE

BORGO

VIA MAZZETTA

To Porta
Romana

To Porta
Romana

the ruler who made the palace (arguably) the center of European culture for a century (c. 1550-1650). Gaze out the windows at the expan-
sive, statue-studded Boboli Gardens, the model for Versailles.

Stroll through palatial rooms with frescoed ceilings and floor-
to-ceiling paintings in gilded frames. In Room 17 you'll run into a fire-
place topped with Lippi's *Madonna and Child* (c. 1452), considered the
first round-framed Renaissance painting.

Continue to the far end, double back, and enter Rooms 27-28,

highlighting Raphael (Raffaelo). His Madonna-and-Childs are dreamy, bathed in even light, with smooth brushwork and restrained colors. By contrast, his portraits are photo-realistic, showing plain faces and human imperfections. Still, everything is geometrically perfect: Women have oval faces, sitters are posed at the best three-quarter angle, and Holy Families stand in pyramid-shaped groups.

Rooms 31-32 focus on the portraits of Titian (Tiziano). With

Lippi's round *Madonna* at the Pitti

Brancacci Chapel, Masaccio's masterwork

rich colors, exuberant motion, and (in later works) rough brushwork, Titian captured Renaissance sophisticates in all their sensual glory. Find his passionate *Mary Magdalene*, the *Portrait of a Man* with piercing blue eyes, and the richly dressed *Portrait of a Lady*.

Included in admission are the Royal Apartments. Ogle rooms of velvety wallpaper, chandeliers, and canopied beds, each a different style and color. Here is the splendor of the Florentine dukes that inspired Europe.

The rest of the complex: It'd be a Pitti to miss the Boboli and Bardini Gardens. See its statue-ringed amphitheater, the melted-frosting Grotto, and the much-photographed fountain of an obese Bacchus.

▶ *To see the Palatine Gallery, Royal Apartments, and Gallery of Modern Art, buy ticket #1—€16 March-Oct (€8 if no special exhibits), lower price off-season, covered by Firenze card. The Palatine is open Tue-Sun 8:15-18:50, closed Mon. The gardens and other museums are €10 March-Oct, lower price off-season, and have similar hours. Tel. 055-238-8614, www.uffizi.beniculturali.it.*

▲▲ Brancacci Chapel

In 1424, 23-year-old Masaccio began frescoing the Brancacci Chapel, where he virtually invented the 3-D realism that defines Western art.

Of the dozen-or-so scenes (mostly about St. Peter), roughly half are by Masaccio and half by his less-talented colleague, Masolino.

In Masaccio's *Adam and Eve* (left wall, upper left), Adam buries his face in shame while Eve wails from deep within. These simple human gestures speak louder than any medieval symbolism.

In *The Tribute Money* (left wall, upper level), Jesus and his

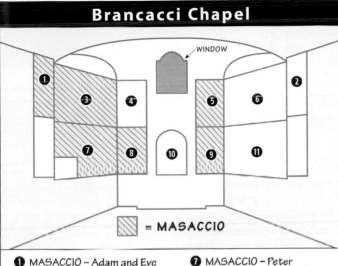

Brancacci Chapel

WINDOW

= MASACCIO

1. MASACCIO – Adam and Eve Banished from Eden
2. MASOLINO – Adam and Eve Tempted by the Serpent
3. MASACCIO – Jesus, Peter & Disciples Pay the Tribute Money
4. MASOLINO – Peter Preaches to a Crowd
5. MASACCIO – Peter Baptizing Converts
6. MASOLINO – Peter Heals a Cripple and Resurrects Tabitha
7. MASACCIO – Peter Resurrects the Son of Theophilus
8. MASACCIO – Peter Heals the Sick with His Shadow
9. MASACCIO – Peter Shares the Wealth with the Poor
10. ANONYMOUS – The Madonna of the People
11. FILIPPINO LIPPI – Peter Crucified

disciples inhabit a spacious world, defined by mountains, the lake, trees, and buildings. They cast late-afternoon shadows to the left, seemingly lit by the same light we are—the natural light from the Brancacci's window. By fixing where we the viewers are in relation to these figures, Masaccio lets us stand in the presence of the human Jesus.

In *Peter Heals the Sick* (center wall, left of window), the saint walks toward us along a Florentine street. Masaccio's people are not generic saints but distinct individuals (like the old bald guy). They exude a seriousness that makes them very adult. Masaccio's ordinary-but-dignified people helped Renaissance-era Florentines shape their own self-image.

Masolino's work, by contrast, reflects an earlier style. The colorful *Peter Heals a Cripple* (right wall, upper level) shows two well-dressed dandies sashaying across a square. Their cardboard-cutout weightlessness, evenly lit cheeriness, and intricately patterned clothes are textbook International Gothic.

Back to Masaccio. Find his self-portrait in *Peter Resurrects the Son of Theophilus* (left wall, lower level). At the far right, Masaccio painted fellow artists Brunelleschi (farthest right, with long black hood), Alberti (slightly to the left), and himself (looking out at us). By the time Masaccio died at 27—the same age as Hendrix, Morrison, Cobain, and Winehouse—he'd rocked the world of art.

▶ *€6, cash only, covered by Firenze Card. Although reservations are required, on weekdays and any day off-season, it's often possible to walk in, especially if you come before 15:30. Open Mon and Wed-Sat 10:00-17:00, Sun 13:00-17:00, closed Tue, last entry 45 minutes before closing. Videoguide-€3. Free 20-minute film has English subtitles. Located in the Church of Santa Maria del Carmine. Reservations tel. 055-276-8224 or 055-276-8558, ticket desk tel. 055-284-361, www.musefirenze.it.*

Santo Spirito Church

Within this church is an interior by Brunelleschi—pure Renaissance. (Ignore the ornate Baroque altar, added later.) Notice Brunelleschi's "dice"—the stone cubes above the column capitals that contribute to the nave's playful lightness.

The church's art treasure is a painted, carved wooden crucifix (*Crocifisso*) by 17-year-old Michelangelo. The sculptor donated this early work to the monastery in appreciation for allowing him to dissect and learn about bodies. It's in the sacristy, which can be accessed through the cloister, entering through the door to the left of the church facade. Copies of Michelangelo's *Pietà* and *Risen Christ* flank the nave (near the main door). Beer-drinking, guitar-playing rowdies decorate the church steps.

▶ *Church-free, open Thu-Tue 10:00-12:30 & 16:00-18:00, Sun from 11:30, closed Wed; cloister-€3, open Mon-Sat 10:00-18:00, Sun 14:00-17:00.*

The view from Piazzale Michelangelo is worth the half-hour hike from Ponte Vecchio.

Located in Piazza di Santo Spirito. Tel. 055-210-030, www.basilica-santospirito.it.

▲ Piazzale Michelangelo

Overlooking the city from across the river, this square with a huge statue of David has a stunning view of Florence. An inviting café is just below the overlook. The best photo-op is from the street immediately below the overlook. Off the west side of the piazza is a quiet terrace. After dark, the square is packed with school kids licking ice cream and each other.

About 200 yards uphill is the stark, beautiful, crowd-free, Romanesque ▲▲**San Miniato Church.** Highlights include the "carpet of marble" floor, a colorful Renaissance tabernacle, the exquisitely painted Chapel of Cardinal Jacopo (left side of the nave), and the tomb of St. Minias (downstairs in the crypt). Upstairs, the sacristy has frescoes (c. 1350) showing St. Benedict—his arm always outstretched—busy blessing, preaching, chasing the devil, and founding his order of monks.

▶ *Take a taxi or bus #12 (20-30 minutes). Then enjoy the easy, pleasant downhill walk back into town: From the piazza (uphill side), take the steps between the two bars and head down Via San Salvatore al Monte.*

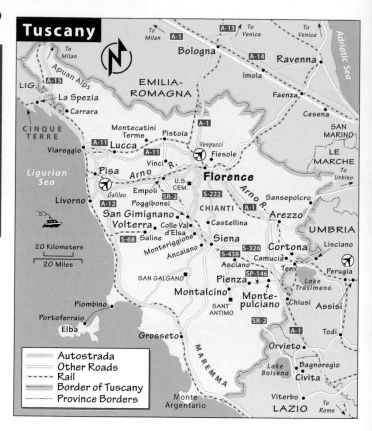

▲Fiesole

Three miles north of downtown Florence, this tiny town perched on a hill overlooking the Arno valley offers great views and a pleasant respite. There's little more to Fiesole (fee-AY-zoh-lay) than a main square (where the bus stops), a few restaurants and shops, a few minor sights...and that great view.

For the best panorama, hike uphill from the main square on Via San Francesco (10 minutes) to the view terrace near La Reggia restaurant. A little farther up is the Church of San Francesco, with colorful altar paintings.

▶ *Getting There: From Florence's Piazza San Marco, take bus #7—past vineyards and villas—to the last stop, Piazza Mino (3-4/hour, fewer after 21:00 and on Sun, 30 minutes, €1.20, €2 if bought on bus). A taxi costs €25-35. The TI is near the main square, behind the Fiesole Duomo at Via Portigiani 3, tel. 055-596-1311, www.fiesoleforyou.it.*

Side Trips from Florence

The following destinations are doable as side-trips from Florence. But they'll be much more satisfying with an overnight or as part of a longer Italian itinerary. For planning tips, see my *Rick Steves Florence & Tuscany* guidebook and my *Rick Steves Rome* guidebook.

Tuscan Hill Towns

Tuscany is speckled with sun- and wine-soaked villages clinging to hilltops, amid rolling farmlands. Of the many sightseeing options, here are a handful of places within 90 minutes of Florence by bus or train. To see more, rent a car.

▲▲▲ **Siena:** This red-brick hilltop city is known for its pageantry, Palio horse race, art-filled Duomo, traffic-free ambience, and stunning main square—great anytime but best after dark. Siena is 90 minutes from Florence by *"rapida/via superstrada"* bus (2/hour), which is faster than the train. For those staying the night in Siena, a hotel-to-hotel taxi ride can be a good value for small groups with luggage (around €120).

▲ **Pisa:** Snap a photo of yourself propping up the iconic Leaning Tower, breeze through the nearby Duomo and Baptistery on the grassy Field of Miracles...and move on. Pisa is an easy hour away on the train.

▲ **Lucca:** Charming city with a lively (and flat) town center, ringed by intact old walls wide enough for biking and strolling. It's 90 minutes by train.

Cortona: This hill town under the Tuscan sun, with historic churches and Etruscan sights, is easily reached by 90-minute direct train from Florence.

▲▲▲ Rome

A 90-minute express train (most require seat reservations) can whisk you into the heart of the Eternal City.

Sleeping

Florence is so compact that all of my recommended hotels are within walking distance of major sights. From Florence's train station, most are a 10- to 15-minute walk or €6-8 taxi ride away. I like hotels that are clean, central, reasonably priced, friendly, small enough to have a hands-on owner and stable staff, and run with a respect for Italian traditions.

Double rooms listed in this book average around €140, ranging from €25 bunks to deluxe €350 doubles. Many Florentine hotels offer a combination of Old World ambience—wood-beam ceilings, frescoes, and antique furniture—with all the modern conveniences.

SLEEPING

Hotel Price Code

$$$$	**Splurge:** Most rooms over €170
$$$	**Pricier:** €130–170
$$	**Moderate:** €90–130
$	**Budget:** €50–90
¢	**Backpacker:** Under €50

These rates are for a standard double room with bath during high season. Unless otherwise noted, breakfast is included, the hotels have an elevator and air-conditioning, and Wi-Fi is generally free.

A Typical Florence Hotel Room

A €140 double room in Florence is small by American standards and has one double bed or two twins. There's probably a private bathroom with a toilet, sink, and bathtub or shower. Rooms generally have a telephone and TV, and may have a safe. Most hotels at this price will have air-conditioning—cheaper places may not. Breakfast is generally included. It's usually a self-service buffet of bread, ham, cheese, yogurt, and juice, while a server takes your coffee order.

The hotel will likely have Internet access, either Wi-Fi or a guest computer in the lobby. The staff speaks at least enough English to get by. Night clerks aren't paid enough to care deeply about problems that arise.

Making Reservations

Reserve your rooms as soon as you've pinned down your travel dates. For busy national holidays, it's wise to reserve far in advance (see page 160). Make reservations by phone, through the hotel's website, or with an email that covers:

- the size of your party and type of rooms you need
- your arrival and departure dates, written European-style— day followed by month and year (for example, 18/06/18 or 18 June 2018); include the total number of nights
- special requests (such as en suite bathroom vs. down the hall, cheapest room, twin beds vs. double bed, quiet room)

- applicable discounts (such as a Rick Steves reader discount, cash discount, or promotional rate)

If they require your credit-card number for a deposit, you can send it by email (I do), but it's safer to share that confidential info via a phone call or fax. Always call or email to reconfirm your room reservation a few days in advance. If you must cancel your reservation, it's polite to do so with as much notice as possible. Cancellation policies can be strict; read the fine print or ask about these before you book.

Budget Tips

Some of my listed hotels offer special rates to my readers—it's worth asking when you book your room.

To get the best deal, contact my family-run hotels directly by phone or email. By going direct, the owner avoids a roughly 20 percent commission and may be able to offer you a discount. Email several hotels to ask for their best price and compare offers—you may be astonished at the range. You may get a better rate if you offer to pay cash, stay at least three nights, skip breakfast, or simply ask if there are any cheaper rooms.

In addition to hotels, I also list a few alternatives. Bed-and-breakfasts (B&Bs) offer a private room in someone's home, often without a 24 hour reception, breakfast room, or public lounge. At nun-run convents, the beds are twins and English is often in short supply, but the price is right. Hostels offer €20-30 dorm beds and a few inexpensive doubles. Airbnb.com makes it reasonably easy to find a place to sleep in someone's home.

Don't be too cheap when picking a hotel. Cheaper places can be depressing, and Florence's intensity is easier to handle with a welcoming oasis to call home. Light sleepers should ask for a *tranquillo* room in the back. In summer, pay a little more for air-conditioning—to avoid both the heat and the mosquitos. If there's no air-conditioning, request a fan and a small plug-in bulb (*zanzariere*) to keep the bloodsuckers at bay.

SLEEPING

THE DUOMO TO THE ARNO RIVER
Central as can be, amid sights and restaurants in the traffic-free core; slightly overpriced but worth it

$$$$ Palazzo Niccolini al Duomo Via dei Servi 2 | tel. 055-282-412 www.niccolinidomepalace.com	Elite historic residence with palatial lounge (free evening tea) and splendid rooms varying wildly in size
$$$$ Hotel Duomo Piazza del Duomo 1 | tel. 055-219-922 www.hotelduomofirenze.it	Modern and comfortable enough; views of Duomo looming like a monster just outside
$$$$ In Piazza della Signoria B&B Via dei Magazzini 2 | tel. 055-239-9546 www.inpiazzadellasignoria.com	Overlooking Piazza della Signoria; peaceful, refined, homey; "partial view" not worth extra
$$$$ Hotel Pendini Via degli Strozzi 2 | tel. 055-211-170 www.hotelpendini.it	Grand, classy-feeling Old World building overlooking Piazza della Repubblica
$$$$ Hotel Davanzati Via Porta Rossa 5 | tel. 055-286-666 www.hoteldavanzati.it	Modern comforts plus artistic touches, cheerfully family-run, evening happy hour, free tablets in every room
$$$$ Hotel Torre Guelfa Borgo S.S. Apostoli 8 | tel. 055-239-6338 www.hoteltorreguelfa.com	Regal public spaces, medieval tower with view, pricey but worth it (especially Room 315)
$$$$ Relais Uffizi Chiasso de Baroncelli/Chiasso del Buco 16 tel. 055-267-6239 www.relaisuffizi.it	Peaceful little gem on alleyway, lounge overlooks magnificent Piazza della Signoria
$$$ Residenza dei Pucci Via dei Pucci 9 | tel. 055-281-886 www.residenzadeipucci.com	13 pleasant rooms, no elevator, aristocratic decor feels upscale for the price
$$$ Soggiorno Battistero Piazza San Giovanni 1 | tel. 055-295-143 www.soggiornobattistero.it	7 simple, pristine rooms; friendly owners, views over Baptistery or quieter rooms in back
$$$ Residenza Giotto B&B Via Roma 6 | tel. 055-214-593 www.residenzagiotto.it	6 bright, slightly scruffy, top-floor rooms on Florence's upscale shopping drag; great view terrace
$$$ Hotel Alessandra Borgo S.S. Apostoli 17 | tel. 055-283-438 www.hotelalessandra.com	Tranquil and sprawling, with 27 big, old-school rooms and tiny Arno-view terrace

$$$ Hotel Maxim Via de' Calzaiuoli 11 | tel. 055-217-474 www.hotelmaximfirenze.it	Straightforward rooms in prime location; painting-lined halls and cozy lounge exude old Florentine charm
$$$ Hotel Axial Via de' Calzaiuoli 11 | tel. 055-218-984 www.hotelaxial.it	Businesslike hotel two floors below its sister Hotel Maxim, comparable rates
$$$ Accademia Rooms Piazza Madonna degli Aldobrandini 1 tel. 055-293-451 www.accademiarooms.com	5 quiet rooms on sunny courtyard, overpriced but convenient location, no elevator
$$ La Residenza del Proconsolo B&B Via del Proconsolo 18 black tel. 066 261 5667 www.proconsolo.com	6 older-feeling rooms, some Duomo views, nice large rooms, breakfast in room, no elevator

NORTH OF THE DUOMO
Not quite so central or picturesque but cheaper, located either near Mercato Centrale or the Accademia

$$$ Hotel Loggiato dei Serviti Piazza S.S. Annunziata 3 tel. 055-289-592 www.loggiatodeiservitihotel.it	Former monastery near Accademia, Old World romance plus modern hair dryers, rickety and characteristic
$$$ Hotel dei Macchiaioli Via Cavour 21 | tel. 055-213-154 www.hoteldeimacchiaioli.com	Fresh and spacious rooms in restored family-run palazzo, frescoed ceilings and modern comfort
$$ Hotel Morandi alla Crocetta Via Laura 50 | tel. 055-234-4747 www.hotelmorandi.it	Former convent on quiet street, period furnishings take you back centuries and up the social ladder
$$ Hotel Europa Via Cavour 14 | tel. 055-239-6715 www.webhoteleuropa.com	Cheery and family-run, spacious breakfast room, most rooms have Duomo views
$$ Relais Grand Tour Via Santa Reparata 21 | tel. 055-283-955 www.florencegrandtour.com	Cozy, artfully appointed B&B makes you feel right at home, spacious suites come with garden ambience, breakfast at corner bar
$$ Galileo Hotel Via Nazionale 22a | tel. 055-496-645 www.galileohotel.it	Comfortable business hotel, well-run with familial warmth, busy street but quiet rooms

$ Hotel Il Bargellino Via Guelfa 87 | tel. 055-238-2658, www.ilbargellino.com	Summery residential ambience, antique furniture and modern paintings, momentum-slowing terrace, no breakfast
$ Casa Rabatti Via San Zanobi 48 black | tel. 055-212-393	Practice your Italian with owner Marcella, the ultimate warm Italian mama; 3 simple, clean rooms; no air-con, no breakfast, cash only
¢ Hostel 7 Santi Viale dei Mille 11 | tel. 055-504-8452, www.7santi.com	"Traveler's haven" filling former convent, best cheap beds in town, take bus #10, #17, or #20 from train station

EAST OF THE DUOMO
Good value conveniently tucked away in an untouristed, unassuming area a few blocks behind the church

$$$ Residenza il Villino Via della Pergola 53 | tel. 055-200-1116 www.ilvillino.it	Quiet refuge with 10 charming rooms and picturesque, peaceful little courtyard
$$$ Panella's Residence Via della Pergola 42 | tel. 055-234-7202 www.panellaresidence.com	Classy B&B in former convent, with 5 chic, romantic, and ample rooms; antique furnishings
$$ B&B Il Bargello Via de' Pandolfini 33 black tel. 055-215-330 www.firenze-bedandbreakfast.it	Small, homey, and Canadian-run; cozy common room, kitchen access, view terrace, no elevator
$$ Locanda de' Ciompi Via Pietrapiana 28 | tel. 055-263-8034 www.bbflorencefirenze.com	Cheap, cheery rooms, nice location, charming idealistic owners; no air-con, breakfast, or elevator
$ Hotel Dalí Via dell'Oriuolo 17 | tel. 055-234-0706 www.hoteldali.com	Cheap, cheery rooms, nice location, charming idealistic owners; no air-con or breakfast, free parking
$ Oblate Sisters of the Assumption Borgo Pinti 15 | tel. 055-248-0582 www.bb-oblate.com	Convent-run old building, dreamy garden and public spaces, simple rooms w/single beds, prayerful ambience

WEST OF THE DUOMO
Efficient location between train station and tourist action, mostly clustered near lively San Lorenzo church

$$$$ Hotel Centrale Via dei Conti 3 | tel. 055-215-761 www.hotelcentralefirenze.it	Midway between station and Duomo, 35 spacious (though overpriced) rooms, tasteful mix of old and new
$$ Bellevue House Via della Scala 21 | tel. 055-260-8932 www.bellevuehouse.it	Oasis of tranquility; 6 spacious, old-fashioned rooms; great budget option, no breakfast or elevator
$$ Albergo Margaret Via della Scala 25 | tel. 055-210-138 www.hotel-margaret.it	7 tidy, simple rooms, homey yet minimalist, no public lounge or breakfast
$ Hotel Lorena Via Faenza 1 | tel. 055-282-785 www.hotellorena.com	Youth-hostel feel, some rooms with bathroom down hall, flexible rates, family-run with care

SOUTH OF THE ARNO RIVER (OLTRARNO)
Farther from the tourists, but nearer to crafts shops, neighborly piazzas, and family eateries

$$$$ Hotel la Scaletta Via de' Guicciardini 13 | tel. 055-283-028 www.hotellascaletta.it	36 pricey, sleek rooms; rooftop terrace overlooking Boboli Gardens; tortured floor plan
$$$ Hotel Silla Via dei Renai 5 | tel. 055-234-2888 www.hotelsilla.it	Classic three-star comfort; 36 cheery, spacious rooms; breezy terrace, faces the river
$ Istituto Gould Via dei Serragli 49 | tel. 055-212-576 www.firenzeforesteria.it	Church-run former palace with garden courtyard; 40 clean, spartan twin rooms; modern facilities, pay extra for air-con
$ Soggiorno Alessandra Via Borgo San Frediano 6 | tel. 055-290-424 www.soggiornoalessandra.it	5 bright, small yet comfy rooms; double-paned windows cut noise, basic breakfast in room, air-con
$ Casa Santo Nome di Gesù Piazza del Carmine 21 | tel. 055-213-856 www.fmmfirenze.it	Convent in big old palace, 25 simple rooms w/twin beds, tranquil garden, no air-con, smiling nuns, 1:00 curfew
↟ Ostello Santa Monaca (Youth Hostel) Via Santa Monaca 6 | tel. 055-268-338 www.ostellosantamonaca.com	Big well-run clean-enough institution attracts young backpackers, 114 beds in 2- to 22-bed dorms

Eating

Florentines are masters of the art of fine eating. Located in the heart of the Tuscan breadbasket, Florence enjoys some of the world's great rustic cuisine. Lingering over a multicourse meal with loved ones while you sip wine from nearby villages...it's one of Florence's great pleasures.

I list a full range of restaurants and eateries—from budget options for a quick bite to multicourse splurges with maximum ambience. I prefer mom-and-pop, personality-driven places, offering fine value and high quality with a local clientele.

When in Florence, I eat on the Florentine schedule. For breakfast, I eat at the hotel or grab a pastry and cappuccino at the neighborhood bar. Lunch is fast and simple to make time for sightseeing—a small sandwich (like many locals), a self-service cafeteria, or a picnic

EATING

Restaurant Price Code

$$$$	**Splurge:** Most main courses over €20
$$$	**Pricier:** €15-20
$$	**Moderate:** €10-15
$	**Budget:** Under €10

Based on the average cost of a typical main course (pasta or secondi). Pizza by the slice and other takeaway food is **$;** a basic trattoria or sit-down pizzeria is **$$;** a casual, more upscale restaurant is **$$$;** and a swanky splurge is **$$$$.**

on a piazza bench. Dinner is the time for slowing down and savoring a restaurant meal. To bridge the gap, people drop into a bar in the late afternoon for a *spuntino* (snack) and aperitif. And then there's gelato...

Restaurants

Restaurants serve lunch from 13:00 to 15:00 (and rarely open their doors before noon). Dinner is served to Florentines after 21:00 and to tourists at 19:00 (quality restaurants rarely open any earlier).

Get used to the reality that many restaurants (even my recommendations) are frequented by fellow tourists—it's inevitable in crowded Florence. Minimize the tourist hordes by eating later, enjoying local ambience at lunchtime (when restaurants cater to office workers), or by escaping to the less-touristed Oltrarno area.

A full restaurant meal comes in courses: appetizer (antipasto), plate of pasta (*primo piatto),* meat or seafood course (*secondo*), salad, dessert, coffee, liqueurs, and so on. It can take hours, and the costs can add up quickly, so plan your strategy before sitting down to a restaurant meal.

For light eaters, there's nothing wrong with ordering a single dish as your meal—a plate of pasta, a pizza, an antipasto, or a salad. Couples could each order a dish (or two) and share. If you want a full meal at a predictable price, consider the *menu turistico*—a fixed-price multi-course meal where you can choose from a list of menu items. It includes the service charge, and is usually a good value for non-gourmets.

In Florence, only rude waiters rush you. For speedier service, be prepared with your next request whenever a waiter happens to grace your table. You'll have to ask for the bill—mime-scribble on your raised palm or ask: *"Il conto?"* Check your bill carefully for additional (dishonest) charges.

Quick Budget Meals

Florence offers many budget options for hungry travelers.

Italian "bars" are cafés, not taverns. These neighborhood hangouts serve coffee, sandwiches (grilled *panini* or cold *tramezzini*), mini-pizzas, pre-made salads, fresh squeezed orange juice (*spremuta*), and drinks from the cooler.

Various cafeteria-style places (called *tavola calda, rosticceria,* or "self-service cafeteria") dish out fast and cheap cooked meals to eat there or take out. You can buy pizza by the slice at little hole-in-the-wall places, sold by weight (100 grams for a small slice). Ethnic joints serve Turkish *döner kebabs* (meat and veggies wrapped in pita bread) and falafel (a fried garbanzo-bean patty). A wine bar (*enoteca*) sells wine by the glass, but they also serve meat-and-cheese-type plates for the business crowd at lunch and happy hour.

At any eating establishment (however humble), be aware that the price of your food and drink may be 20-40 percent more if you consume it while sitting at a table instead of standing at the bar. This two-tier price system will always be clearly posted. Don't sit without first checking out the financial consequences. At many bars, the custom is to first pay the cashier for what you want, then hand the receipt to a barista who serves you.

Picnicking saves euros and time, lets you sample regional specialties, and puts you in contact with everyday Florentines in the marketplace. Buy a sandwich or slice of pizza "to go" (*da portar via*), get fruit at the corner grocery store (*supermercato*), pick up a bottle of wine, refill your water bottle at a public tap...and dine like a Medici amid atmospheric surroundings. Florence's large covered farmers market, the Mercato Centrale (see page 116), is a picnic-shopper's paradise. When buying produce, it's customary to let the merchant pick it out. If something is a mystery, ask for a small taste—*"Un assaggio, per favore?"*

Florentine Cuisine

Along with the basic dishes you'll find all over Italy, Florence has its signature specialties. Florentine cuisine is hearty, simple farmers'

Gelato

The Florentines claim they invented gelato, or Italian-style ice cream. Many think it's the world's best. Gelato uses slightly less milk fat than American-style ice cream, letting the natural flavors come through. It's generally homemade on the premises, proudly advertised as *artiginale, nostra produzione,* or *produzione propia.*

Check the price board listing the different sizes of cups and cones. Choose your container (for example, "a €3 cone" or "a €4 cup"), then point out the flavors you want. They'll let you put more than one flavor in even the smallest container.

Try free samples before ordering—*"Un assaggio, per favore?"* (oon ah-SAH-joh pehr fah-VOH-ray). Ask the server which flavors go well together—*"Quali gusti stanno bene insieme?"* (KWAH-lee GOO-stee STAH-noh BEH-nay een-see-EH-may). Afficionados avoid the bright, chemical-colored flavors that draw children. Don't limit your tasting to a single *gelateria.* When it comes to gelato in Florence, I say, *"Perchè no?"*—Why not?

food: grilled meats, high-quality vegetables in season, fresh herbs, prized olive oil, beans, and rustic bread.

For appetizers, try *panzanella,* a summery tomato salad with bread chunks, or pecorino cheese, made from ewe's milk. *Ribollita* is a bean soup. A classic main dish is *bistecca alla fiorentina,* a steak grilled very rare (and sold expensively by the gram—confirm the total price). Florentines love fresh game, such as boar *(cinghiale)* or game birds. *Spiedino* is roast meats on a skewer. Anything described as *"...alla fiorentina"* (in the Florentine style) usually means it's cooked with vegetables, especially spinach. Florentines traditionally eat lots of tripe *(trippa)*—intestines—as good as it sounds.

No meal in Italy is complete without wine. Even the basic house wine *(vino da tavola or vino della casa)* is fine with a meal. Tuscany is world-renowned for producing hearty Sangiovese-grape reds that pair well with meat dishes. The famous Chianti wine is grown 20 miles south of Florence. More complex (and expensive) is Brunello di Montalcino, or its cheaper cousin, Rosso di Montalcino. Vino Nobile di Montepulciano is a dry ruby red that's much better than the "Montepulciano" wine sold in US grocery stores. The so-called "Super

Tuscans" are a creative new breed of wines made from non-native grapes now grown in Italy. For a crisp white, try Orvieto Classico.

Italian coffee is some of the world's best. Even the most basic hole-in-the-wall bar serves quality espresso, *macchiatos,* and cappuccinos. In summer, Florentines like a sugared iced coffee called *caffè freddo.*

Popular liqueurs to finish a meal are *amaro* (various brands) and anise-flavored Sambuca. Florentines love dipping biscotti in *vin santo* (literally "holy wine"), a sweet, golden dessert wine. Or pick up a cup or cone of gelato at a *gelateria* and stroll the streets with the rest of Florence, enjoying a bit of edible art.

THE DUOMO TO THE ARNO RIVER
Historic, atmospheric, overpriced, and touristy—better to just grab a quick lunch while sightseeing

❶	**$ Self-Service Ristorante Leonardo** Via Pecori 11 tel. 055-284-446	Inexpensive, air-conditioned, quick, a block southwest of Baptistery, hardworking staff, free water (daily 11:45-14:45 & 18:45-21:45)
❷	**$$$$ Frescobaldi Ristorante and Wine Bar** Via dei Magazzini 2 red tel. 055-284-724	Aristocratic, formal, candlelit ambience and great wine, dress-up dinners, more casual lunch (daily 12:00-14:30 & 19:00-22:30)
❸	**$$ Cantinetta dei Verrazzano** Via dei Tavolini 18 red tel. 055-268-590	Sandwich plates and wine in old-time setting, light meals for office workers, delicious cakes (Mon-Sat 8:00-21:00, Sun 10:00-16:30)
❹	**$$ Osteria Vini e Vecchi Sapori** Via dei Magazzini 3 red tel. 055-293-045	Colorful hole-in-the-wall restaurant serving Tuscan food, fun and accessible, reserve for dinner (Mon-Sat 12:30-14:30 & 19:30-22:30, closed Sun)
❺	**$ I Fratellini** Via dei Cimatori tel. 055-239-6096	Informal, longstanding sandwich-and-cheap-wine eatery, order something exotic, sit on curb with locals (daily 9:00-19:30 or until the bread runs out)
❻	**$ Il Cernacchino** Via della Condotta 38 red tel. 055-294-119	Handy, well-regarded shop selling panino sandwiches (Mon-Sat 9:30-19:30, closed Sun)

EATING

NORTH OF THE DUOMO
Better value than the historic center, but still many fellow tourists. Find these near the Mercato Centrale or the Accademia.

7	**$$$ La Ménagère Bistro and Restaurant** Via de' Ginori 8 red tel. 055-075-0600	Fun, high-energy place serves Tuscan specialties to happy tourists, arrive early or make reservation, check bill carefully (daily 11:00-23:00)
8	**$$ Trattoria Mario's** Via Rosina 2 tel. 055-218-550	Lunch-only local fixture, bustling service, home cooking, good value, shared tables, arrive early, cash only (Mon-Sat 12:00-15:30, closed Sun and Aug)
9	**$$ Trattoria la Burrasca** Via Panicale 6 tel. 055-215-827	Small friendly Flintstone-chic eatery, good-value seasonal home cooking, popular with my readers (Tue-Sun 12:00-15:00 & 19:00-22:30, closed Mon)
10	**$$ Pepò** Via Rosina 4 red tel. 055-283-259	Colorful, charmingly unpretentious neighborhood eatery serving simple yet well-prepared Florentine classics (daily 12:00-14:30 & 19:00-22:30)
11	**$-$$ Mercato Centrale** (Central Market) Just north of the Church of San Lorenzo	Upstairs: gleaming foodie mecca with a dozen upscale food counters and restaurants (daily 10:00-24:00). Ground floor: market zone filled with raw ingredients, picnic delicacies, and humble food counters (Mon-Fri 7:00-14:00, Sat 7:00-17:00, closed Sun)
11	**$ Nerbone in the Market** Inside Mercato Centrale	Inside the Mercato Centrale, venerable diner for cheap sit-down meal with fellow shoppers, cash only (lunch menu served Mon-Sat 12:00-14:00, sandwiches from 8:00 until the bread runs out, closed Sun)
12	**$ Casa del Vino** Via dell'Ariento 16 red tel. 055-215-609	Well-regarded wine shop serves small sandwiches to mobs of locals on lunch break (Mon-Sat 9:30-20:30 year-round, closed Sun year-round, Sat in summer, and Aug)
13	**$$ Pasticceria Robiglio** Via dei Servi 112 red tel. 055-212-784	Near the Accademia, elegant little café, limited menu but generous spirit (daily 12:00-15:00, longer hours as a café)

| ⑭ | **$ La Mescita Flaschetteria**
Via degli Alfani 70 red
mobile 338-992-2640 | Untouristed student-filled hole-in-the-wall; pasta, sandwiches, cheap wine; point to what you want, check your bill (Mon-Sat 11:30-15:30, closed Sun) |
| ⑮ | **Carrefour Express**
Via Riascoli 109 red | Handy supermarket with sandwich counter and picnic supplies, eat on historic Piazza S.S. Annunziata (daily 8:00-20:00) |

EAST OF THE DUOMO
Find these between the Palazzo Vecchio and Santa Croce Church

⑯	**$$ Ristorante del Fagioli** Corso dei Tintori 47 tel. 055-244-285	Proud, enthusiastic family serves loyal customers home-style classics, reserve for dinner, cash only (Mon-Fri 12:00-14:00 & 19:00-22:30, closed Sat-Sun)
⑰	**$ All'Antico Vinaio** Via dei Neri 65 red tel. 055-238-2723	Florentine favorite, offers stand-up wining and sandwich dining, sit-down place across the street (Mon-Sat 10:30-22:30, Sun 12:00-16:00)
⑱	**$$ Trattoria Anita** Corner of Via Vinegia and Via del Parlagio at 2 red tel. 055-218-698	Wood paneling and rows of wine bottles, three-course weekday lunch specials (Mon-Sat 12:00-14:30 & 19:00-22:15, closed Sun)
⑲	**$$ Trattoria I'cche C'è C'è** Via Magalotti 11 red tel. 055-216-589	EE-kay chay chay; "whatever there is, there is," small mom-and-pop place, cozy and welcoming, functional Florentine dishes (Tue-Sun 12:30-14:30 & 19:30-22:30, closed Mon)

WEST OF THE DUOMO
Near the church of Santa Maria Novella

⑳	**$$ Trattoria al Trebbio** Via delle Belle Donne 47 red tel. 055-287-089	Traditional food (rabbit, steak), simple candlelit elegance inside or outside on romantic square (daily 12:00-15:00 & 19:00-23:00)
㉑	**$$ Trattoria "da Giorgio"** Via Palazzuolo 100 red tel. 055-284-302	Family-style home cooking makes a fun night out for happy locals and tourists, fixed-price meal a great value (Mon-Sat 12:00-14:30 & 18:30-22:00, closed Sun)
㉒	**$$ Trattoria Marione** Via della Spada 27 red tel. 055-214-756	Sincerely cooked home-style meals in crowded, happy atmosphere beneath hanging ham hocks (daily 12:00-17:00 & 19:00-23:00)

㉓	**$$$ Trattoria Sostanza-Troia** Via del Porcellana 25 red tel. 055-212-691	Famous for (splittable) steaks and pastas, crowded, shared tables, reserve for dinner, cash only (lunch Mon-Sat 12:30-14:00, dinner seatings at 19:30 and 21:00, closed Sun year-round and Sat off-season)
㉔	**$$ Procacci** Via Tornabuoni 64 red tel. 055-211-656	Swanky wine bar specializes in truffle-scented ingredients; reasonably priced sandwiches, pricey sampler plates (daily 10:00-21:00)

SOUTH OF THE ARNO RIVER (OLTRARNO)
More out-of-the-way but more authentic. Florentines may even outnumber my readers.

㉕	**$$$ Golden View Open Bar** Via dei Bardi 58 tel. 055-214-502	Ponte Vecchio view; lively trendy bistro for romantic meal or just salad, pizza, or pasta with fine wine; reserve for window, jazz lounge drinks (18:30-21:30) include free appetizers (daily 12:00-24:00)
㉖	**$$$ Il Santo Bevitore Ristorante** Via di Santo Spirito 64 tel. 055-211-264	Dark and dressy tables, creative Tuscan cuisine paired with wine, come early or reserve (daily 12:30-14:30 & 19:30-22:30, closed Mon for lunch)
㉗	**$$$ Trattoria 4 Leoni** Via de' Vellutini 1 tel. 055-218-562	Quintessential Oltrarno scene on colorful square, traditional but creative food, good house wine, reservations wise (daily 12:00-24:00)
㉘	**$$$ Antico Ristoro Di' Cambi** Via Sant'Onofrio 1 red tel. 055-217-134	Meat lover's dream, rustic bustling beer-hall energy, confirm full price of your sold-by-weight *bistecca* (Mon-Sat 12:00-14:30 & 18:30-22:30, closed Sun)
㉙	**$ Trattoria Sabatino** Via Pisana 2 red tel. 055-225-955	Untouristed, spacious, brightly lit mess hall; little English, simple menu, disturbingly cheap (Mon-Fri 12:00-14:30 & 19:15-22:00, closed Sat-Sun)
㉚	**$$ Signorvino** Via dei Bardi 46 red tel. 055-286-258	Enoteca (wine shop) with simple restaurant with rare terrace over Arno River, no pretense, quality Italian ingredients, fine meats and cheeses (daily 9:30-24:00, food served 11:30-23:00)
㉛	**$$$$ Olio & Convivium Gastronomia** Via di Santo Spirito 4 tel. 055-265-8198	Romantic and a little pretentious, for well-dressed foodies, good-value sampler plates, wines by the glass, air-con (Tue-Sun 12:00-14:30 & 19:00-22:30, closed Mon)

Hearty rustic cuisine is a Florentine speciality, and meat is its centerpiece.

32	**$$ Trattoria Al Tranvai** Piazza Torquato Tasso 14 red tel. 055-225-197	Locals cram into dark-wood tables, like a small town's favorite eatery (Mon 19:00-24:00, Tue-Sat 12:30-14:30 & 19:30-22:30, closed Sun)
33	**$$ Trattoria Casalinga** Via de' Michelozzi 9 red tel. 055-218-624	Aproned women bustle serving hordes of Florentines and happy tourists, near colorful Santo Spirito (Mon-Sat 12:00-14:30 & 19:00-22:00, closed Sun and Aug)
34	**$$ Tamerò** Piazza di Santo Spirito 11 red tel. 055-282-596	Arty pasta bar in old auto mechanic's shop serving quality Sardinian-Tuscan dishes (daily 12:00-late)

Florence Restaurants

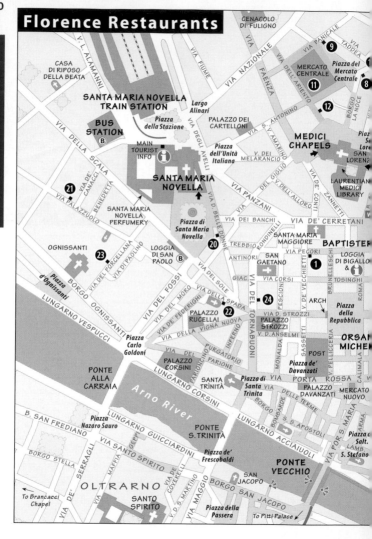

To San Marco Museum

UNIVERSITY

VIA GIUSEPPE GIUSTI

VIA SAN GALLO
VIA GUELFA

15

ACCADEMIA (DAVID)

SANT. ANNUNZIATA

Piazza S.S. Annunziata

VIA LAURA

VIA DELLA COLONNA

BORGO PINTI

LEONARDO MUSEUM

7

i

MEDICI-RICCARDI PALACE

VIA RICASOLI

MUSEUM OF PRECIOUS STONES

14 **13**

V. D. ALFANI

HOSPITAL OF THE INNOCENTS

300 Meters

300 Yards

V. D. COLONNA

VIA DEI SERVI

PALAZZO PUCCI

VIA DEL PINTI
VIA DEI BIGHI

i ROTUNDA

Piazza Brunelleschi

LEONARDO MUSEUM

DUOMO & BAPT. TICKETS

VIA M. BUFALINI

HOSPITAL

VIA DELLA PERGOLA

VIA NUOVO DI CACCINI

BORGO PINTI

VIA PILASTRI

DUOMO MUSEUM

DUOMO

Piazza di Santa Maria Nuova

MUSEO DI FIRENZE COM'ERA

VIA S. EGIDIO

VIA FIESOLANA

Piazza del Duomo

CAMPANILE

CANONICA

VIA DELL'OGHE

A DELL'OGHE

STUDIO

OPERA DEL DUOMO STUDIO

VIA DELL'ORIUOLO

VIA DI MEZZO

SANTA MARIA DE' RICCI

VIA DEL CORSO

i CASA DI DANTE

BORGO DEGLI ALBIZI

Piazza G. Salvemini

VIA PIETRAPIANA

POST

VIA DELL'ULIVO

TAVO.

VIA D. ALIGHIERI

V. DE' PANDOLFINI

VIA DEL PROCONSOLO

VIA DE' GERALDI

VIA DELL'AGNOLO

S. MARIA LA BADIA

5 CIM.

BARGELLO MUSEUM

VIA DELLA VIGNA VECCHIA

VIA BURELLA

V. PALCHIERI

STINCHE

GHIBELLINA

VIA G. VERDI

CASA BUONARROTI

VIA GHIBELLINA

NDOTTA

2

6

Piazza S. Firenze

VIA DELL'ANGUILLARA

BENTA

VERRAZZANO

V. DEL FICO

VIA DI DEPEI

zza della gnoria

GONDI

4

PALAZZO VECCHIO

BORGO DE' GRECI

VIA LEONI

CORNO

Piazza Peruzzi

Piazza Santa Croce

VIA DI SAN GIUSEPPE

GIA

UFFIZI GALLERY

18 **19**

VINEGIA

MAGALOTTI

RUSTICI

VIA D. BENCI

WC

SANTA CROCE

i

17

CASTELANI

OSTERIA

VIA DE' NERI

BR.CHE

PAZZI CHAPEL

Piazza Giudici

SAPONAIO

Piazza Mentana

VAGELLA

MALENCHINI

CORSO DEI TINTORI

LIBRARY

GALILEO SCIENCE MUS.

LUNG. GEN. DIAZ

16

To ㉘ & ㉙

PONTE AL
CARRAI

Ⓑ
#12

Piazza
Nazaro
Sauro

LUNGAR

LA CITÉ
LIBRERIA CAFÉ

BORGO SAN FREDIANO

㉖

Piazza
degli Scarla

VIA SANTO SPIRITO

VIA SANTO SPIRITO

VIA DEL LEONE

To Porta
San Frediano

VIA DELL'ORTO

Piazza del
Carmine

BORGO STELLA

SANTA
MONACA

VIA SANTA MONACA

BRANCACCI
CHAPEL

SANTA MARIA
DEL CARMINE

VIA DE' SERRAGLI

VIA MAFFIA

OLTR

To ㉜

VIA S. AGOSTINO

Piazza di
Santo Spirito

❸

PAL. DE
COSIMO
RIDOLFI

V. MAZZETTA

VIA DEL CAMPUCCIO

VIA DELLA CHIESA

V. D. CALDAIE

Giardino
Torrigiani

200 Meters

200 Yards

To Porta
Romana

VIA DE' SERRAGLI

Giardino
di Analena

VIA ROMANA

Oltrarno Restaurants

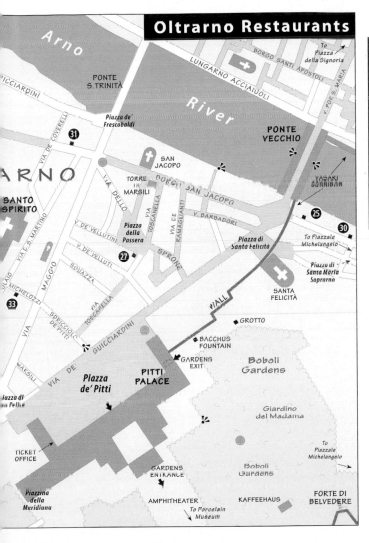

Arno

PONTE S.TRINITÀ

LUNGARNO ACCIAIUOLI

BORGO SANTI APOSTOLI

To Piazza della Signoria

River

TICCIARDINI

Piazza de' Frescobaldi

31

VIA DE' COVERELLI

V. POR S. MARIA

PONTE VECCHIO

SAN JACOPO

ARNO

VIA DELLO

TORRE DE MARSILI

BORGO SAN JACOPO

VIA TOSCANELLA

VIA DE' RAMAGLIANTI

V. BARBADORI

VASARI CORRIDOR

SANTO SPIRITO

V. DE' VELLUTINI

Piazza della Passera

V. DE' VELLUTI

SPRONE

Piazza di Santa Felicità

25

30

To Piazzale Michelangelo

27

VIA L. S. MARTINO

VIA S. MARTINO

MAGGIO

SQUAZZA

VIA TOSCANELLA

Piazza di Santa Maria Soprarno

MICHELOZZI

33

VIA

SPRUGGIOLO DE' PITTI

VIA DE GUICCIARDINI

VIALE

SANTA FELICITÀ

GROTTO

BACCHUS FOUNTAIN

Boboli Gardens

MARSILI

iazza di n Felice

Piazza de' Pitti

PITTI PALACE

GARDENS EXIT

Giardino del Madama

TICKET OFFICE

GARDENS ENTRANCE

To Piazzale Michelangelo

Piazzina della Meridiana

AMPHITHEATER

To Porcelain Museum

Boboli Gardens

KAFFEEHAUS

FORTE DI BELVEDERE

Practicalities

PLANNING

Tuscany's best travel months (also its busiest and most expensive) are April, May, June, September, and October. These months combine the convenience of peak season with pleasant weather. July and August sizzle with temperatures into the 90s (get a hotel with air-conditioning). November to March (with temperatures in the 40s and 50s) have none of the sweat and stress of the tourist season, but sights may have shorter hours. Even off-season, Florence can be crowded on holiday weekends. Any time of year, many sights are closed on Monday and close early on Sunday.

Make sure your passport is up to date (to renew, see www.travel.state.gov). Call your debit- and credit-card companies about your plans (see later). Book hotel rooms in advance, especially for travel during peak season or holiday weekends. Consider buying travel insurance (see www.ricksteves.com/insurance). If traveling beyond Florence, research transit schedules (trains, buses) and car rentals. If renting a car, you're technically required to have an International Driving Permit (sold at your local AAA office), though I've often rented cars in Italy without one. Consider making reservations for key sights (see page 166). Get a current list of museum hours at www.firenzeturismo.it.

MONEY

Italy uses the euro currency: 1 euro (€) = about $1.20. To convert euros to dollars add about 20 percent: €20 = about $24, €50 = about $60. (Check www.oanda.com for the latest exchange rates.)

Withdraw money from an ATM (known as a *bancomat* in Italy) using a debit card, just like at home. Visa and MasterCard are commonly used throughout Europe. Before departing, call your bank and credit-card company: Ask about international transaction fees, alert them that you'll be making withdrawals in Europe, and if you don't know it, get your credit card PIN. Many travelers bring a second debit/credit card as a backup. Many Italian merchants prefer cash, so withdraw large amounts (€250-300) from the ATM.

While American credit cards are accepted almost everywhere in Europe, even newer chip-style cards may not work in some payment machines (e.g., ticket kiosks). If your card is rejected, be prepared to

Helpful Websites

Italian Tourist Information: www.italia.it

Florence Tourist Information: www.firenzeturismo.it

Cheap Flights: www.kayak.com (for international flights), www.skyscanner.com (for flights within Europe)

European Train Schedules: www.bahn.com

General Travel Tips: www.ricksteves.com (trip planning, packing lists, and more—plus updates for this book)

pay with cash, find a nearby cashier who can swipe it, or try entering your PIN.

To keep your valuables safe, wear a money belt. But if you do lose your credit or debit card, report the loss immediately with a collect phone call: Visa (tel. 303/967-1096), MasterCard (tel. 636/722-7111), and American Express (tel. 623/492-8427).

ARRIVAL IN FLORENCE

Amerigo Vespucci Airport (a.k.a. Peretola)

Florence's airport is about five miles northwest of the city. Though small, it has all the services you'd expect—a TI, ATMs, car-rental agencies, cafés, and shops (airport code: FLR, no overnighting allowed, airport info tel. 055-306-1830, www.aeroporto.firenze.it).

To get between the airport and downtown, you have two main options:

Taxi: You'll pay €22 for the 20-30-minute ride during the day, €25.30 at night, and €24 on Sunday.

Shuttle Buses: These connect the airport (departing from the far right as you exit the arrivals hall) with Florence's train and bus stations (described later; from the bus station, it's a 20-minute walk to the Duomo, or take a city bus or taxi). Airport shuttle buses depart twice an hour daily 5:00-00:30, and take 30 minutes (€6—buy your ticket on board).

Santa Maria Novella Train Station

Florence's main train station (called Firenze S.M.N. to distinguish it from Florence's two smaller stations) is on the western edge of the historic center, an easy 10- to 15-minute walk to the Duomo.

With your back to the tracks, get oriented. To the left is baggage storage (halfway down track 16). Directly ahead—outside the station—is a TI, located straight across the square, 100 yards away. To the right (also outside the station) is the handy Sapori & Dintorni Conad supermarket, for sandwiches and salads to go. Avoid long ticket-window lines by using the easy-to-master ticket machines, or use a travel agency near your hotel.

To get into town, exit the station to the left. There you'll find taxis (€6-8 to the Duomo) and city buses (buy tickets at the small ATAF ticket office inside main station hall). To walk into town, exit the station straight ahead, through the main hall, and head straight across the square outside (toward the Church of Santa Maria Novella). On the far side of the square, keep left and head down Via dei Panzani, which leads directly to the Duomo.

BusItalia Bus Station

Located 100 yards west of the Florence S.M.N. train station on Via Santa Caterina da Siena, this is the hub for regional buses to Siena, San Gimignano, and other Tuscan hill towns, plus the shuttle bus to and from Florence's Amerigo Vespucci Airport. For most buses, buy tickets in the station, or pay 30 percent more if you pay on board. Bus service drops dramatically on Sunday. Bus info: Tel. 800-373-760 or www.fsbusitalia.it.

To walk into town, exit the station through the main door, and turn left along the busy street toward the brick dome. The train station is on your left, while downtown Florence is straight ahead and a bit to the right.

Tips for Drivers

Don't drive into the city center. Strictly enforced laws ticket those without a permit who enter the *Zona Traffico Limitato*. Instead, park your car at one of several big parking lots on the perimeter, where you can catch a bus or taxi into the center. Find a lot (*"trova parcheggio"*) at www.firenzeparcheggi.it.

Arrival by Cruise Ship at the Port of Livorno

The coastal town of Livorno is about 60 miles west of Florence. A day-trip into Florence is doable but busy, involving at least two hours of round-trip travel. To do it on your own by bus-and-train is, frankly, too much trouble. The easiest option is to book an excursion through your cruise line. Or, hire a private taxi or minibus—these are waiting at the dock as travelers disembark. They'll drive you into Florence (one-hour trip), give you about five hours of sightseeing time, then bring you back to the port. Establish a total price beforehand and pay at the end.

HELPFUL HINTS

Tourist Information (TI): At any TI, pick up a current listing of museum hours. This is very important, because hours can change from month to month (or download the current list at www.firenzeturismo.it). TIs also have city maps, but many hotels do, too. The TIs at the train station and on Via Cavour sell the Firenze Card (see page 165).

The main TI sits 100 yards directly across the square from the **train station,** but it's very crowded (Piazza della Stazione 4, Mon-Sat 9:00-19:00, Sun until 14:00, tel. 055-212-245, www.firenzeturismo.it). Another branch is next to the **Duomo** (west corner of Via de' Calzaiuoli, inside Loggia, same hours as train station branch). A third TI is a couple of blocks **north of the Duomo** (Via Cavour 1 red, Mon-Fri 9:00-13:00, closed Sat-Sun, tel. 055-290-832).

Hurdling the Language Barrier: Many Italians—especially those in the tourist trade and in big cities—speak English. Still, learn the pleasantries such as *buon giorno* (good day), *mi scusi* (pardon me), *per favore* (please), *grazie* (thank you), and *arrivederci* (goodbye). For more Italian survival phrases, see page 173.

Time Zones: Italy is generally six/nine hours ahead of the East/West coasts of the US.

Business Hours: Smaller stores are generally open about 9:00-13:00 and 15:30-19:30, usually closed on Sunday, often closed on Monday (or at least Monday morning), and sometimes closed for a couple of weeks around August 15. Bigger stores have similar hours, without the afternoon break. Department stores stay open later and on Sunday.

Watt's Up? Europe's electrical system is 220 volts, instead of North America's 110 volts. You'll need an adapter plug with two round prongs, sold inexpensively at travel stores in the US. Most newer electronics (such as mobile devices, laptops, hair dryers, and battery chargers) convert automatically, so you won't need a separate converter.

Numbers and Stumblers: What Americans call the second floor of a building is the first floor in Europe. Europeans write dates as day/month/year, so Christmas is 25/12/19. Commas are decimal points and vice versa—a dollar and a half is $1,50, and there are 5.280 feet in a mile.

Italy uses the metric system: A kilogram is 2.2 pounds; a liter is about a quart; and a kilometer is six-tenths of a mile. Temperature is measured in Celsius. 0°C = 32°F. To roughly convert Celsius to Fahrenheit, double the number and add 30.

Holidays: Many sights and banks close down on national holidays. Verify dates at www.italia.it or www.firenzeturismo.it, or check www.ricksteves.com/festivals.

Addresses: Florence has a ridiculously confusing system for street addresses. They use "red" numbers (e.g., Via Cavour 2r) for businesses, and "black" numbers (e.g., Via Cavour 25n) for residences. I'm lazy and don't concern myself with the distinction—if one number's wrong, I look nearby for the other.

Wi-Fi: Nearly all Florence hotels have Wi-Fi free for guests, and many cafés and restaurants will tell you their password if you buy something. The city's free Wi-Fi hotspot network covers all of the main squares (network name is "Firenze WiFi"—click on *"Accedi"*; good for two hours).

Bookstores: You can pick up cheap, pretty-good art-and-history guidebooks at kiosks and museums. For English books and guidebooks (including mine), try Paperback Exchange (south of the Duomo at Via delle Oche 4 red) or RED (on Piazza della Repubblica).

Laundry: The Wash & Dry Lavarapido chain has self-service launderettes at several locations: Via dei Servi 105 red (near David), Via del Sole 29 red and Via della Scala 52 red (between train station and river), Via Ghibellina 143 red (Palazzo Vecchio), and Via dei Serragli 87 red (Oltrarno). Most are open daily 7:30-23:00.

Free Water: Carry a water bottle to refill at twist-the-handle public fountains, like the one to the left of Palazzo Vecchio.

Tipping

Tipping in Europe isn't as automatic and generous as it is in the US. At Italian restaurants that have waitstaff, a "service" charge (servizio) of about 10 percent is usually included in your bill. Italians don't tip beyond this, but if the service is exceptional, you can round up the bill by a euro or two. At hotels, it's polite to give porters a euro for each bag (another reason to pack light). To tip a taxi driver, round up to the nearest euro (for a €5.50 fare, give €6), or up to 10 percent for longer rides.

Services: WCs are scarce. Use them when you can, in any café or museum you patronize.

Be Ready: Though small, Florence is intense. Prepare for scorching summer heat, slick pickpockets, few WCs, steep prices, and long lines. Easy tourist money has corrupted some locals, making them greedy and dishonest (check your bill carefully).

GETTING AROUND FLORENCE

Because Florence is so compact, I walk everywhere. I mainly use buses to reach outlying sights (Piazzale Michelangelo or Fiesole) and taxis to shuttle me and my bags between the hotel and the train station/airport.

On Foot: I think of Florence as my Renaissance treadmill—it requires a lot of walking. Much of the historic core is pedestrian-only, but it's still an intense urban environment of narrow streets, tourist crowds, and busy locals speeding through on bicycles and motorbikes.

Buses: A single ticket is €1.20, good for 90 minutes. A 24-hour pass is €5, and Firenze Card holders ride free. Buy tickets at tobacco shops (tabacchi), newsstands, the ATAF ticket windows inside the train station, or sometimes on board for a bit more (€2, exact change). Validate your ticket in the machine on board. Most buses leave from two major hubs: the train station or Piazza San Marco (near the Accademia). For bus information, get a transit map at the TI, call 800-424-500, or check www.ataf.net.

I find these to be most helpful bus lines:

#C2 twists through the congested old center from the train station, passing near Piazza della Repubblica and Piazza della Signoria to Piazza Beccaria.

#C1 stops behind the Palazzo Vecchio and Piazza Santa Croce, then heads north to Piazza Libertà.

#D goes from the train station to Ponte Vecchio, then cruises through the Oltrarno (passing Pitti Palace) as far east as Ponte San Niccolò.

#12 go from the train station to the Oltrarno, Piazzale Michelangelo, and San Miniato Church. Bus #13 makes the return trip down the hill.

#7 goes from Piazza San Marco (near the Accademia) to Fiesole (small town with views).

Taxi: The minimum cost is €5 (€8.30 after 22:00, €7 on Sun). Taxi fares and supplements are clearly explained on signs in each taxi—rides in the center of town should be charged as tariff #1. A typical taxi ride from the train station to the Duomo costs about €8. It can be hard to hail a cab on the street. To call one, dial 055-4390 or 055-4242.

Bike Rental: The city of Florence rents bikes cheaply (€2/hour, €10/day) at the train station. Get info at a TI or tel. 346-883-7821.

STAYING CONNECTED

You can bring your own mobile device (phone, tablet, laptop) and follow my budget tips. Or buy a European SIM card for your phone. Or just use European landlines (in your hotel room) and computers (there's usually one in your hotel lobby). These three options are described in full at www.ricksteves.com/phoning.

Making Calls

To **call Italy from a US or Canadian phone:** Dial 011 (international access code), 39 (Italy' country code), and the phone number.

To **call Italy from a European phone:** Dial 00, then 39 followed by the phone number.

To **make calls within Italy:** If you're dialing from an Italian mobile phone or landline to another, simply dial the phone number, including the initial 0 if there is one.

To **call from Italy to another country:** Dial 00, the country code, and then the number.

Initial Zero: Drop the initial zero from international phone numbers—except when calling Italy.

Mobile Tip: Pressing the + sign auto-selects the correct international access code.

Using Your Mobile Device in Europe

Use free Wi-Fi whenever possible. Unless you have an unlimited data plan, save most of your online tasks for Wi-Fi. Many hotels and cafés have Wi-Fi for guests.

Sign up for an international plan. Most providers offer a global plan that cuts the cost of calls and texts, and gives you a block of data. Your normal plan may already include international coverage.

Minimize the use of your cellular network. If you can't find Wi-Fi, you can roam on your cellular network. When you're done, avoid further charges by disabling cellular data or roaming in your settings. Save bandwidth-gobbling tasks (Skyping, downloading apps, streaming) for when you're on Wi-Fi.

Use calling/messaging apps for cheaper calls and texts. Some apps (Skype, Viber, FaceTime, Google+ Hangouts) let you call or text for free or cheap when you're on Wi-Fi.

Buy a European SIM card. This option helps you get faster data connections and make voice calls at cheap local rates. Buy a basic phone in Europe (about $40 from a phone shop) or bring an "unlocked" US phone from home. Once you insert a European SIM, you'll have a European phone number. Buy a new card when you arrive in a new country (sold at phone shops, newsstands, vending machines, and department-store electronics counters). In Italy, tourists should buy SIM cards at mobile-phone shops. You'll be required to register the SIM card with your passport as an antiterrorism measure, which may mean you can't use the phone for the first hour or two.

Stick to landlines. If it's inexpensive to make calls from your hotel-room phone (ask at the desk for rates before you dial), you can make your calls even cheaper by using an international phone card (sold at many newsstands, street kiosks, tobacco shops, and train stations).

PRACTICALITIES

Useful Contacts

English-Speaking Police Help: Tel. 113

Ambulance: Tel. 118

US Embassy (in Rome): 24-hour emergency line—tel. 06-46741, non-emergency—tel. 06-4674-2420, http://italy.usembassy.gov

US Consulate (in Florence): Tel. 055-266-951, http://florence.usconsulate.gov

Canadian Embassy (in Rome): Tel. 06-854-442-911, www.italy.gc.ca

SIGHTSEEING TIPS

Plan Ahead to Avoid Crowds: Avoid long ticket-buying lines at major sights by making reservations, buying a Firenze Card, or buying combo-tickets (these options are described in more detail later in this section). This is especially necessary from April through October and on all holiday weekends.

Hours: Check opening hours carefully and plan your time well. Some sights have erratic hours (e.g., closed the second and fourth Monday of the month). Hours can change season-to-season, so get the most up-to-date list from a TI or at www.firenzeturismo.it. Many sights are closed Monday and have shorter hours Sunday. You may not be allowed to enter if you arrive less than 30-60 minutes before closing time, and guards start shooing people out before the closing time, so don't save the best for last.

What to Expect: Important sights have metal detectors or conduct bag searches that will slow your entry. Some don't allow large bags or don't allow you to bring liquids (water bottles) in. Photos and videos are normally allowed, but flashes or tripods usually are not.

Dress Code at Churches: Some sights are also churches, and they may enforce a modest dress code—no shorts, bare shoulders, or miniskirts. You'll find this at the Duomo, Santa Maria Novella, Santa Croce, and the Medici Chapels. Some churches sell cheap, disposable ponchos for instant respectability. Other churches encourage a dress code but don't enforce it. Churches that aren't major sights usually close from around 12:30 to 15:30.

Discounts: Many sights offer discounts for seniors, families, and students or teachers with proper identification cards (www.isic.org). Always ask. Children under 18 sometimes get in for free or cheap. Some discounts are only for EU citizens.

Pace Yourself: Schedule cool breaks into your sightseeing where you can sit and refresh with a drink or snack.

🎧 **Free Rick Steves Audio Tours:** I've produced free audio tours covering some of Florence's best sights, including the Renaissance Walk and tours of the Accademia, Uffizi Gallery, Bargello, and Museum of San Marco. You can download Rick Steves Audio Europe via Apple's App Store, Google Play, or the Amazon Appstore.

Firenze Card

The Firenze Card (€72) is pricey but convenient. This three-day sightseeing pass gives you admission to many of Florence's sights, including the Uffizi Gallery, the Accademia, and the Duomo-related sights. Just as important, it lets you skip the ticket-buying lines without making reservations (except for the Duomo dome climb). For busy sightseers, the card can save some money. And for anyone, it can certainly save time.

With the card, you simply go to the entrance, find the Firenze Card priority line, show the card, and they let you in.

Add up your sightseeing to see if it's worth it: Uffizi Gallery (as much as €24 with temporary exhibits plus reservation fee) + Accademia (€16.50 with reservation fee) + Bargello (€8) + Medici Chapels (€8) + Palazzo Vecchio (€10), and so on. Factor in the time saved waiting in ticket lines, and the freedom to pop into lesser sights you otherwise wouldn't pay to visit. If you're planning to see five or six major sights in a short time, the card pays for itself.

You can buy the card at many participating museums. The least-crowded outlet is the TI a couple of blocks north of the Duomo at Via Cavour 1 red. To get the most from your card, validate it only when you're ready to tackle the covered sights in 72 consecutive hours (e.g., 15:00 Tue until 15:00 Fri). Note that not all of Florence's sights are covered. For a complete list of included sights, see www.firenzecard.it.

Advance Reservations

If you decide not to get a Firenze Card, you can avoid ticket lines by making reservations (€4 per ticket booking fee) at key sights. I recommend them for the Uffizi Gallery (book weeks or months in advance) and the Accademia (a few days ahead is usually enough). Off-season (Nov-March), you can usually enter without significant lines after 16:00. There are several ways to make a reservation:

• **Through Your Hotel:** When you make your hotel reservation, ask if they can book your museum reservations, too.

• **By Phone:** From a US phone, dial 011-39-055-294-883 to reach an English-speaking operator who walks you through the process in a few minutes. The booking office is open Mon-Fri 8:30-18:30, Sat 8:30-12:30, closed Sun. The line is often busy, so be persistent.

• **Online:** Using a credit card, you can book through the city's official site, www.firenzemusei.it (€4/ticket reservation fee). More user-friendly are booking sites www.uffizi.com or www.tickitaly.com, but their fees are steep—about €10 per ticket.

• **Reserve in Florence:** If you arrive without a reservation, try the booking window at Orsanmichele Church (daily 9:00-16:00) or the My Accademia Libreria bookstore across from the Accademia (Tue-Sun 8:15-17:30).

Combo-Ticket for the Duomo and Related Sights

Five Duomo-related sights are covered by a €15 combo-ticket (no individual tickets): the Duomo's dome, Campanile, Baptistery, Duomo Museum, and Duomo crypt. (Admission to the Duomo itself is free.) You can buy tickets at the office opposite the Baptistery entrance, and at the Campanile, Duomo crypt, and Duomo Museum (lines at the museum are usually the shortest). Tickets are not sold at the dome. Even with a combo-ticket (or Firenze Card), to climb the dome, you'll need a reservation (best to book online well in advance).

Uffizi/Pitti Palace/Boboli Gardens Combo-Ticket

Valid for three consecutive days, this combo-ticket offers a cost-saving one-time priority (skip-the-line) admission to the Uffizi Gallery, Pitti Palace, and Boboli Gardens (€38 March-Oct, €18 Nov-Feb, not valid first Sun of the month when admission is free; www.uffizi.it).

THEFT AND EMERGENCIES

Theft: While violent crime is rare in the city center, thieves (mainly pickpockets) thrive in crowds. Be alert to the possibility of theft, even when you're absorbed in the wonder and newness of Florence. Be on guard whenever crowds press together, while you're preoccupied at ticket windows, anywhere around major sights, and while boarding and leaving buses. Be especially alert around Florence's train station, the station's underpass (and where the tunnel surfaces), and at major sights. Assume that any beggar or friendly petitioner is really a pickpocket, and any commotion in the crowd is a distraction by a team of thieves.

I keep my valuables—passport, credit cards, crucial documents, and large amounts of cash—in a money belt that I tuck under my belt-line. Dial 113 for English-speaking police help. To replace a passport, contact an embassy or consulate (for contact info, see page 164). File a police report without delay; it's required to submit an insurance claim for lost or stolen rail passes or travel gear, and can help with replacing your passport or credit and debit cards. For more information, see www.ricksteves.com/help.

Medical Help: Dial 113 for English-speaking police/medical emergencies, or 118 for an ambulance. If you get sick, do as the Italians do and go to a pharmacy, where qualified technicians routinely diagnose and prescribe. Or ask at your hotel for help—they'll know the nearest medical and emergency services. English-speaking doctors include Medical Service Firenze (tel. 055-475-411, www.medicalservice.firenze.it) or Dr. Stephen Kerr (tel. 055-288-055, mobile 335-836-1682, www.dr-kerr.com).

ACTIVITIES

Shopping

Florence is a great shopping town, known for its sense of style since the Medici days. It offers the full range, from glitzy high-fashion boutiques to haggle-till-you-drop street markets. Many smaller stores use siesta hours—open Monday to Saturday 9:00-13:00 and 15:30-19:30, usually closed on Sunday, and often closed on Monday.

High-Fashion Boutiques: The entire area between the Duomo and the Arno River bristles with trendy fashion boutiques. The Gucci Museum (€7, but may be closed), right on Piazza della Signoria, tells the story of that famous designer. Ponte Vecchio houses gold and silver shops. The upscale La Rinascente department store is on Piazza della Repubblica.

Via de' Tornabuoni, three blocks west of Piazza della Repubblica, is especially classy, home to the Ferragamo handbag-and-shoe store (Via de' Tornabuoni 2) and its nearby shoe museum (Piazza Santa Trinità 5). Also nearby, check out Via degli Strozzi, Via della Vigna Nuova, and Via del Parione.

Markets: Every day, the **San Lorenzo Market** (see page 115) offers stalls of touristy goods (leather bags, T-shirts, trinkets) in the streets just north of the Basilica of San Lorenzo. Close by is the large covered market known as the **Mercato Centrale,** which contains an upscale food court and food and produce vendors (see page 116). **Mercato Nuovo** (three blocks north of Ponte Vecchio) is an open-air loggia with souvenir items (see page 108). In the **Santa Croce area** (southeast of the Duomo), the Piazza dei Ciompi flea market runs daily, but only really hops on the last Sunday of the month. The area hosts several bargain leather stores and the pricey leather school inside Santa Croce Church (see page 118). South of the river in the **Oltrarno,** find antique and artisan shops near the Pitti Palace on Via Romana and Sdrucciolo de' Pitti, and near the river on Borgo San Jacopo and Via di Santo Spirito.

Souvenir Ideas: You won't need a guidebook to find all kinds of art-themed posters, calendars, Botticelli mouse pads, Raphael lipstick-holders, and plaster *David*s. With its history as a literary center, Florence offers traditional marbled stationery, leather-bound journals, fine pens, and reproductions of old manuscripts. Tuscan hand-painted ceramics are popular. Italian foods—olives, cheese, pesto—must conform to US Customs rules (see next page). Bringing fragile bottles of Italian wine home in your luggage is legal but can be a recipe for disaster.

Sizes: European clothing sizes are different from the US. For example, a woman's size 10 dress (US) is a European size 40, and a size 8 shoe (US) is a European size 38-39.

Getting a VAT Refund: If you spend more than €155 on goods at a single store, you may be eligible to get a refund of the 22 percent

Value-Added Tax (VAT). You'll need to ask the merchant to fill out the necessary refund document, then process your refund through a service such as Global Blue or Premier Tax Free, with offices at major airports. For more details, see www.ricksteves.com/vat.

Customs for American Shoppers: You are allowed to take home $800 worth of items per person duty-free, once every 31 days. You can also bring home one liter of alcohol duty-free. As for food, you can take home many processed and packaged foods (e.g., vacuum-packed cheeses, chocolate, mustard). Fresh produce and most meats are not allowed. Any liquid-containing foods must be packed (carefully) in checked luggage. To check customs rules and duty rates, visit http://help.cbp.gov.

If You Go Overboard: To bring all of your booty home, you can buy a cheapo suitcase (for as little as €25) at the stalls outside the Church of Santa Maria Novella, opposite the train station.

Entertainment and Nightlife

For me, nighttime is for eating a late meal, catching a concert, strolling through the old town with a gelato, or hitting one of the many pubs. Find English language films at the Odeon Cinema (near Piazza della Repubblica on Piazza Strozzi, tel. 055-214-068, www.odeonfirenze.com). Get the latest on nightlife and concerts from *The Florentine* magazine (free from the TI) or *Firenze Spettacolo* (bought from newsstands), or check www.firenzespettacolo.it or www.firenzeturismo.it.

Stroll from the Duomo to the Arno: Join the parade of locals on their evening *passegiata*, strolling the pedestrian zone, enjoying cafés, *gelaterie,* great people-watching, and street performers. Pop into a wine bar *(enoteca)* to sample regional wines by the glass or a plate of meats and cheeses. (Psst. Near the Duomo, find La Congrega Lounge Bar—a tiny retreat on a tiny lane just off the main pedestrian drag, at Via Tosinghi 3 red.) End at the Arno, to stand atop Ponte Vecchio and watch the sun set, the moon rise, and lovers kiss. Other great nighttime scenes are the viewpoints at Piazzale Michelangelo (page 129) and in Fiesole (page 130).

Live Music: Orsanmichele Church, in the heart of Florence's historic core, hosts chamber music under its Gothic arches. Tickets are sold on the day of the concert from the door facing Via de' Calzaiuoli. Orchestra della Toscana, near the Bargello, presents major classical concerts from November to May (Via Ghibellina 97, tel. 055-210-804, www.orchestradellatoscana.it). St. Mark's English Church, south of the Arno, offers opera (Via Maggio 18, mobile 340-811-9192, www.concertoclassico.info). Golden View Open Bar, a river-view restaurant near Ponte Vecchio, has live jazz three nights a week at 21:00 (see page 148). Boxoffice Toscana sells tickets for rock concerts and more (Via delle Vecchie Carceri 1, tel. 055-210-804, www.boxofficetoscana.it).

Late-Night Partying: With so many American and international college students in town, Florence by night can have a frat-party atmosphere. Piazza Santa Croce and bars along nearby Via de' Benci are the epicenter of international-student partying, with occasional rock concerts in the square. For a more local crowd, head south from Santa Croce across the river (crossing Ponte alle Grazie) to find a few late-night bars at Piazza Demidoff. In the Oltrarno southwest of Ponte Vecchio, Piazza di Santo Spirito is trendy and bohemian but also seedy.

Guided Tours

Hop-On Hop-Off Bus Tours: Double-decker buses give tourists a drive-by look at major landmarks while listening to recorded descriptions. But since many important sights are in the pedestrian-only historic core, Florence doesn't really lend itself to this kind of tour—check out the route map before committing (€23 for one calendar day, pay as you board, www.firenze.city-sightseeing.it).

Walking and Bicycle Tours: Many companies offer English-language, 2- to 3-hour small-group tours of Florence's sights, for around €25-75 a person. Some offer a Rick Steves discount—it's worth asking.

ArtViva Walking Tours offers a variety of tours of the town, the main museums, day trips, bike tours, and cooking classes (office is near Piazza della Repubblica at Via de' Sassetti 1, tel. 055-264-5033 www.artviva.com). Florencetown Tours does walking tours, biking tours, and cooking classes (near Palazzo Vecchio at Via de Lamberti 1, tel. 055-281-103, www.florencetown.com). For a more scholarly approach, try Walks Inside Florence (mobile 335-526-6496, www.walksinsideflorence.com), Florentia (www.florentia.org), or Context Florence (tel. 06-9672-7371, US tel. 800-691-6036, www.contexttravel.com).

If you'd like a private guide (around €70/hour), consider Alessandra Marchetti (mobile 347-386-9839, alessandramarchettitours@gmail.com) or Paola Migliorini (mobile 347-657-2611, www.florencetour.com).

Florentine cooking classes dish up fun and tasty hands-on experiences.

Cooking Classes, Art-Making, and More: Most of the tour companies listed earlier also offer Florence experiences. I've enjoyed cooking classes, a paint-your-own-fresco art class, food-oriented walks, Tuscan day trips, lectures, kids' programs, wine tours, and more. Check their websites.

RESOURCES FROM RICK STEVES

This Pocket guide is one of dozens of titles in my series of guide-books on European travel. I also produce a public television series, *Rick Steves' Europe,* and a public radio show, *Travel with Rick Steves.* My website, www.ricksteves.com, offers a wealth of free travel information, including videos and podcasts of my shows and classes, audio tours of Europe's great sights, travel forums, guidebook updates, and information on European rail passes—plus an online travel store and information on our tours of Europe.

How Was Your Trip? You can share your tips, concerns, and discoveries at www.ricksteves.com/feedback. I value your feedback. Thanks in advance.

Italian Survival Phrases

English	Italian	Pronunciation
Good day.	Buon giorno.	bwohn JOR-noh
Do you speak English?	Parla inglese?	PAR-lah een-GLAY-zay
Yes. / No.	Si. / No.	see / noh
I (don't) understand.	(Non) capisco.	(nohn) kah-PEES-koh
Please.	Per favore.	pehr fah-VOH-ray
Thank you.	Grazie.	GRAHT-seeay
You're welcome.	Prego.	PRAY-go
I'm sorry.	Mi dispiace.	mee dee-speeAH-chay
Excuse me.	Mi scusi.	mee SKOO-zee
(No) problem.	(Non) c'è un problema.	(nohn) cheh oon proh-BLAY-mah
Good.	Va bene.	vah BEHN-ay
Goodbye.	Arrivederci.	ah-ree-vay-DEHR-chee
one / two	uno / due	OO-noh / DOO-ay
three / four	tre / quattro	tray / KWAH-troh
five / six	cinque / sei	CHEENG-kway / SEHee
seven / eight	sette / otto	SEHT-tay / OT-toh
nine / ten	nove / dieci	NOV-ay / deeAY-chee
How much is it?	Quanto costa?	KWAHN-toh KOS-tah
Write it?	Me lo scrive?	may loh SKREE-vay
Is it free?	È gratis?	eh GRAH-tees
Is it included?	È incluso?	eh een-KLOO-zoh
Where can I buy / find...?	Dove posso comprare / trovare...?	DOH-vay POS-soh kohm-PRAH-ray / troh-VAH-ray
I'd like / We'd like...	Vorrei / Vorremmo...	vor-REHee / vor-RAY-moh
...a room.	...una camera.	OO-nah KAH-meh-rah
...a ticket to ___.	...un biglietto per ___.	oon beel-YEHT-toh pehr
Is it possible?	È possibile?	eh poh SEE bee-lay
Where is...?	Dov'è...?	DOH-veh
...the train station	...la stazione	lah staht-seeOH-nay
...the bus station	...la stazione degli autobus	lah staht-seeOH-nay DAYL-yee OW-toh-boos
...tourist information	...informazioni per turisti	een-for-maht-seeOH-nee pehr too-REE-stee
...the toilet	...la toilette	lah twah-LEHT-tay
men	uomini, signori	WOH-mee-nee, seen-YOH-ree
women	donne, signore	DON-nay, seen-YOH-ray
left / right	sinistra / destra	see-NEE-strah / DEHS-trah
straight	sempre diritto	SEHM-pray dee-REE-toh
When do you open / close?	A che ora aprite / chiudete?	ah kay OH-rah ah-PREE-tay / keeoo-DAY-tay
At what time?	A che ora?	ah kay OH-rah
Just a moment.	Un momento.	oon moh-MAYN-toh
now / soon / later	adesso / presto / tardi	ah-DEHS-soh / PREHS-toh / TAR-dee
today / tomorrow	oggi / domani	OH-jee / doh-MAH-nee

In the Restaurant

I'd like...	Vorrei...	vor-REHee
We'd like...	Vorremmo...	vor-RAY-moh
...to reserve...	...prenotare...	pray-noh-TAH-ray
...a table for one / two.	...un tavolo per uno / due.	oon TAH-voh-loh pehr OO-noh / DOO-
Non-smoking.	Non fumare.	nohn foo-MAH-ray
Is this seat free?	È libero questo posto?	eh LEE-bay-roh KWEHS-toh POH-stol
The menu (in English), please.	Il menù (in inglese), per favore.	eel may-NOO (een een-GLAY-zay) pehr fah-VOH-ray
service (not) included	servizio (non) incluso	sehr-VEET-seeoh (nohn) een-KLOO-z
cover charge	pane e coperto	PAH-nay ay koh-PEHR-toh
to go	da portar via	dah POR-tar VEE-ah
with / without	con / senza	kohn / SEHN-sah
and / or	e / o	ay / oh
menu (of the day)	menù (del giorno)	may-NOO (dayl JOR-noh)
specialty of the house	specialità della casa	spay-chah-lee-TAH DEHL-lah KAH-za
first course (pasta, soup)	primo piatto	PREE-moh peeAH-toh
main course (meat, fish)	secondo piatto	say-KOHN-doh peeAH-toh
side dishes	contorni	kohn-TOR-nee
bread	pane	PAH-nay
cheese	formaggio	for-MAH-joh
sandwich	panino	pah-NEE-noh
soup	minestra, zuppa	mee-NEHS-trah, TSOO-pah
salad	insalata	een-sah-LAH-tah
dessert	dolci	DOHL-chee
tap water	acqua del rubinetto	AH-kwah dayl roo-bee-NAY-toh
mineral water	acqua minerale	AH-kwah mee-nay-RAH-lay
milk	latte	LAH-tay
(orange) juice	succo (d'arancia)	SOO-koh (dah-RAHN-chah)
coffee / tea	caffè / tè	kah-FEH / teh
wine	vino	VEE-noh
red / white	rosso / bianco	ROH-soh / beeAHN-koh
glass / bottle	bicchiere / bottiglia	bee-keeAY-ray / boh-TEEL-yah
beer	birra	BEE-rah
Cheers!	Cin cin!	cheen cheen
More. / Another.	Ancora un po.' / Un altro.	ahn-KOH-rah oon poh / oon AHL-troh
The same.	Lo stesso.	loh STEHS-soh
The bill, please.	Il conto, per favore.	eel KOHN-toh pehr fah-VOH-ray
tip	mancia	MAHN-chah
Delicious!	Delizioso!	day-leet-seeOH-zoh

For more user-friendly Italian phrases, check out *Rick Steves' Italian Phrase Book Dictionary* or *Rick Steves' French, Italian, and German Phrase Book*.

INDEX

Start your trip at

Our website enhances this book and turns

Explore Europe

At ricksteves.com you can browse through thousands of articles, videos, photos and radio interviews, plus find a wealth of money-saving travel tips for planning your dream trip. And with our mobile-friendly website, you can easily access all this great travel information anywhere you go.

TV Shows

Preview the places you'll visit by watching entire half-hour episodes of Rick Steves' Europe (choose from all 100 shows) on-demand, for free.

ricksteves.com

your travel dreams into affordable reality

Radio Interviews

Enjoy ready access to Rick's vast library of radio interviews covering  travel tips and cultural insights that relate specifically to your Europe travel plans.

Travel Forums

Learn, ask, share! Our online community of savvy travelers is a great resource for first-time travelers to Europe, as well as seasoned pros. You'll find forums on each country, plus travel tips and restaurant/hotel reviews. You can even ask one of our well-traveled staff to chime in with an opinion.

Travel News

Subscribe to our free Travel News e-newsletter, and get monthly updates from Rick on what's happening in Europe.

Audio Europe™

Rick's Free Travel App

Get your FREE Rick Steves Audio Europe™ app to enjoy...

- Dozens of self-guided tours of Europe's top museums, sights and historic walks
- Hundreds of tracks filled with cultural insights and sightseeing tips from Rick's radio interviews
- All organized into handy geographic playlists
- For Apple and Android

With Rick whispering in your ear, Europe gets even better.

Find out more at ricksteves.com

Pack Light and Right

Gear up for your next adventure at ricksteves.com

Light Luggage

Pack light and right with Rick Steves' affordable, custom-designed rolling carry-on bags, backpacks, day packs and shoulder bags.

Accessories

From packing cubes to moneybelts and beyond, Rick has personally selected the travel goodies that will help your trip go smoother.

Shop at ricksteves.com

Rick Steves has

Save time and energy

This guidebook is your independent-travel toolkit. But for all it delivers, it's still up to you to devote the time and energy it takes to manage the preparation and logistics that are essential for a happy trip. If that's a hassle, there's a solution.

Rick Steves Tours

A Rick Steves tour takes you to Europe's most interesting places with great guides and small groups

great tours, too!

with minimum stress

of 28 or less. We follow Rick's favorite itineraries, ride in comfy buses, stay in family-run hotels, and bring you intimately close to the Europe you've traveled so far to see. Most importantly, we take away the logistical headaches so you can focus on the fun.

Join the fun

This year we'll take thousands of free-spirited travelers—nearly half of them repeat customers—along with us on four dozen different itineraries, from Ireland to Italy to Istanbul. Is a Rick Steves tour the right fit for your travel dreams? Find out at ricksteves.com, where you can also request Rick's latest tour catalog.

Europe is best experienced with happy travel partners. We hope you can join us.

See our itineraries at ricksteves.com

A Guide for Every Trip

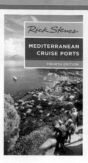

BEST OF GUIDES

Full color easy-to-scan format, focusing on Europe's most popular destinations and sights.

Best of France
Best of Germany
Best of England
Best of Europe
Best of Ireland
Best of Italy
Best of Spain

COMPREHENSIVE GUIDES

City, country, and regional guides with detailed coverage for a multi-week trip exploring iconic sights and more.

Amsterdam & the Netherlands
Barcelona
Belgium: Bruges, Brussels, Antwerp & Ghent
Berlin
Budapest
Croatia & Slovenia

Eastern Europe
England
Florence & Tuscany
France
Germany
Great Britain
Greece: Athens & the Peloponnese
Iceland
Ireland
Istanbul
Italy
London
Paris
Portugal
Prague & the Czech Republic
Provence & the French Riviera
Rome
Scandinavia
Scotland
Spain
Switzerland
Venice
Vienna, Salzburg & Tirol

Rick Steves guidebooks are published by Avalon Travel,
an imprint of Perseus Books, a Hachette Book Group company.

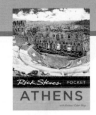

AMSTERDAM **ATHENS** **BARCELONA** **LONDON**

POCKET GUIDES

Amsterdam
Athens
Barcelona
Florence
Italy's Cinque Terre
London

Munich & Salzburg
Paris
Prague
Rome
Venice
Vienna

SNAPSHOT GUIDES

Focused single-destination coverage.

Basque Country: Spain & France
Copenhagen & the Best of Denmark
Dublin
Dubrovnik
Edinburgh
Hill Towns of Central Italy
Krakow, Warsaw & Gdansk
Lisbon
Loire Valley
Madrid & Toledo
Milan & the Italian Lakes District
Naples & the Amalfi Coast
Northern Ireland
Normandy
Norway
Reykjavik
Sevilla, Granada & Southern Spain
St. Petersburg, Helsinki & Tallinn
Stockholm

CRUISE PORTS GUIDES

Reference for cruise ports of call.

Mediterranean Cruise Ports
Northern European Cruise Ports

TRAVEL SKILLS & CULTURE

Europe 101
European Christmas
European Easter
European Festivals
Europe Through the Back Door
Postcards from Europe
Travel as a Political Act

PHRASE BOOKS & DICTIONARIES

French
French, Italian & German
German
Italian
Portuguese
Spanish

PLANNING MAPS

Britain, Ireland & London
Europe
France & Paris
Germany, Austria & Switzerland
Ireland
Italy
Spain & Portugal

Rick Steves books are available from your favorite bookseller.
Many guides are available as ebooks.

PHOTO CREDITS

Cover
Santa Maria del Fiore Cathedral
© Susanne Kremer / Huber Images / eStock Photo

Title Page
Ponte Vecchio © Dominic Arizona Bonuccelli

Accademia Tour
Page 40, top, Donatello—David (bronze, c. 1430) Bargello
© Art Kowalsky / Alamy

Page 40, bottom, Andrea del Verrocchio—David (c. 1470) Bargello
© SuperStock / Alamy

Page 41, bottom, Gian Lorenzo Bernini—David (c. 1623) Borghese
Museum, Rome © Art Kowalsky / Alamy

Page 45, right, Michelangelo—*Pietà* © Ivy Close Images / Alamy

Bargello Tour
Page 80, left, Andrea del Verrocchio—David (c. 1470) Bargello
© SuperStock / Alamy

Page 80, right, Donatello—David (bronze, c. 1430) Bargello
© Art Kowalsky / Alamy

Page 82, left, Donatello—Niccolò da Uzzano (c. 1420)
© The Print Collector / Alamy

Page 82, right, Donatello—St. George (S. Giorgio, 1416)
© DK Images / Alamy

Page 84, Ghiberti and Brunelleschi—Baptistery Door Competition
Entries, titled Abraham Sacrificing Isaac (Sacrificio di Isacco, 1401)
© Peter Barritt / Alamy

Duomo Museum Tour

Page 91, left, Ghiberti—Adam and Eve (La Creazione e Storie di Adamo ed Eva) panel © Kumar Sriskandan / Alamy

Page 91, right, Ghiberti—Labors of Adam, and Cain and Abel ('Il Lavoro dei Progenitori e Storie di Caino e Abele) panel Duomo Museum © Richard Osbourne / Alamy

Page 92, left, Ghiberti—Joseph and Benjamin (Storie di Giuseppe e Beniamino) panel Duomo Museum ©Skim New Media Limited p/ Alamy

Page 92, right, Ghiberti—Solomon and the Queen of Sheba (Salomone e la Regina di Saba) panel Duomo Museum © Ugo Cei / Alamy

Avalon Travel
Hachette Book Group
1700 Fourth Street
Berkeley, CA 94710, USA

Printed in China by RR Donnelley
ISBN 978-1-63121-825-5
Third Edition
First printing June 2018

For the latest on Rick's lectures, guidebooks, Europe tours, public television series, and public radio show, contact Rick Steves' Europe, 130 Fourth Avenue North, Edmonds, WA 98020, tel. 425/771-8303, www.ricksteves.com, rick@ricksteves.com.

Rick Steves' Europe
Managing Editor: Jennifer Madison Davis
Special Publications Manager: Risa Laib
Assistant Managing Editor: Cathy Lu
Editors: Glenn Eriksen, Tom Griffin, Katherine Gustafson, Suzanne Kotz, Carrie Shepherd
Editorial & Production Assistant: Jessica Shaw
Editorial Intern: Alexandra Ivy
Researcher: Sarah Murdoch
Graphic Content Director: Sandra Hundacker
Maps & Graphics: David C. Hoerlein, Lauren Mills, Mary Rostad

Avalon Travel
Senior Editor and Series Manager: Madhu Prasher
Editor: Jamie Andrade
Associate Editor: Sierra Machado
Copy Editor: Maggie Ryan
Proofreader: Kelly Lydick
Indexer: Stephen Callahan
Production & Typesetting: Christine DeLorenzo
Cover Design: Kimberly Glyder Design
Maps & Graphics: Kat Bennett, Mike Morgenfeld
Additional Photography: Dominic Arizona Bonuccelli, Ben Cameron, Cameron Hewitt, Gene Openshaw, Rick Steves, Laura VanDeventer, Wikimedia Commons (PD-Art/PD-US).
Photos are used by permission and are the property of the original copyright owners.

Although the author and publisher have made every effort to provide accurate, up-to-date information, they accept no responsibility for loss, injury, overcooked pasta, or inconvenience sustained by any person using this book.

ABOUT THE AUTHORS

Rick Steves

Since 1973, Rick has spent about four months a year exploring Europe. His mission: to empower Americans to have European trips that are fun, affordable, and culturally broadening. Rick produces a best-selling guidebook series, a public television series, and a public radio show, and organizes small-group tours that take over 20,000 travelers to Europe annually. He does all of this with the help of a hardworking, well-traveled staff of 100 at Rick Steves' Europe in Edmonds, Washington, near Seattle. When not on the road, Rick is active in his church and with advocacy groups focused on economic justice, drug policy reform, and ending hunger. To recharge, Rick plays piano, relaxes at his family cabin in the Cascade Mountains, and spends time with his partner Trish, son Andy, and daughter Jackie. Find out more about Rick at www.ricksteves.com and on Facebook.

Gene Openshaw

Gene has co-authored a dozen *Rick Steves* books, specializing in writing walks and tours of Europe's cities, museums, and cultural sights. He also contributes to Rick's public television series, produces tours for Rick Steves Audio Europe, and is a regular guest on Rick's public radio show. Outside of the travel world, Gene has co-authored *The Seattle Joke Book*. As a composer, Gene has written a full-length opera called *Matter* (soundtrack available on Amazon), a violin sonata, and dozens of songs. He lives near Seattle with his daughter, enjoys giving presentations on art and history, and roots for the Mariners in good times and bad.

FOLDOUT COLOR MAP

The foldout map on the opposite page includes:

• **A map of Florence on one side**
• **Maps of Tuscany on the other side**